THE GREAT

WESTERN CANADA

BUCKET LIST

The Great Canadian Bucket List Series

The Great Western Canada Bucket List
The Great Canadian Bucket List
The Great Northern Canada Bucket List
The Great Canadian Prairies Bucket List
The Great Central Canada Bucket List
The Great Atlantic Canada Bucket List

ROBIN ESROCK

THE GREAT

WESTERN CANADA

BUCKET LIST

One-of-a-Kind Travel Experiences

Second Edition

DUNDURN
PRESS

Publisher: Kwame Scott Fraser | Acquiring editor: Kathryn Lane | Editor: Jess Shulman
Cover and interior designer: Laura Boyle | Front cover image: TJ Watt | Back cover image: Pursuit | Original maps: Mary Rostad

Library and Archives Canada Cataloguing in Publication

Title: The Great Western Canada Bucket List : one-of-a-kind travel experiences / Robin Esrock.
Names: Esrock, Robin, 1974- author.
Description: Second edition. | Series statement: The great Canadian bucket list ; 2 | Includes index.
Identifiers: Canadiana (print) 20230567290 | Canadiana (ebook) 20230567347 | ISBN 9781459753938 (softcover) | ISBN 9781459753945 (PDF) | ISBN 9781459753952 (EPUB)
Subjects: LCSH: Esrock, Robin, 1974-—Travel—Alberta. | LCSH: Esrock, Robin, 1974-—Travel—British Columbia. | LCSH: Alberta—Guidebooks. | LCSH: British Columbia—Guidebooks. | LCSH: Alberta—Description and travel. | LCSH: British Columbia—Description and travel. | LCGFT: Guidebooks.
Classification: LCC FC3657 .E86 2024 | DDC 917.1204/4—dc23

We acknowledge the support of the Canada Council for the Arts and the Ontario Arts Council for our publishing program. We also acknowledge the financial support of the Government of Ontario, through the Ontario Book Publishing Tax Credit and Ontario Creates, and the Government of Canada.

Care has been taken to trace the ownership of copyright material used in this book. The author and the publisher welcome any information enabling them to rectify any references or credits in subsequent editions.

The publisher is not responsible for websites or their content unless they are owned by the publisher.

Dundurn Press
1382 Queen Street East
Toronto, Ontario, Canada M4L 1C9
dundurn.com, @dundurnpress

For my father, Joe Kalmek, who's more at home in his forests and mountains than anywhere else.

CONTENTS

ALBERTA

LAND ACKNOWLEDGEMENT

ACTIVITIES AND DESTINATIONS IN THIS BOOK TAKE PLACE ON the traditional territories and lands of the Indigenous Peoples in British Columbia and Alberta. As such, it's important to recognize and honour the deep connection they have with this land, their home since time immemorial. While I've been fortunate to explore both provinces extensively, I am grateful to make my own home on the unceded traditional territories of the Coast Salish (Musqueam, Squamish, and Tsleil-Waututh Nations).

In British Columbia, I'd like to further acknowledge the traditional territories of many Indigenous Peoples, including but not limited to the Nuu-chah-nulth, Kwakwaka'wakw, Haida, Secwépemc, Ktunaxa, Nuxalk, Gitga'at Lax Yuup, Syilx Okanagan, Cayuse, Umatilla, Walla Walla, and Stó:lō.

In Alberta, I acknowledge that these lands are the traditional territories of many Indigenous Peoples, including but not limited to the Blackfoot Confederacy (Siksika, Peigan-Piikani, and Kainai-Blood Tribe), Stoney Nakoda (Chiniki, Bearspaw, and Goodstoney), Tsuut'ina, Cree, Dene, Métis, and Sioux (Nakota, Dakota, and Lakota).

As visitors, I hope we can honour and respect their rights, cultures, and traditional territories, and engage with their wisdom and teachings. There is a lot to learn, and we should do so responsibly and thoughtfully, following sustainable tourism practices as we connect with each community in an authentic, positive manner. Most of all, I have strived — as I hope you do — to travel with gratitude, engaging diverse landscapes, people, creatures, histories, and culture with an open heart and an open mind.

INTRODUCTION

AN AUSTRALIAN TOURIST IS TELLING ME ALL ABOUT HIS vacation in Western Canada.* We are descending in a carriage on the Sea to Sky Gondola, enjoying a star attraction in a region full of them. The teal waters of Howe Sound glitter below in the late afternoon sun.

"I thought I lived in God's Country, and then I came here," he exclaims, with a heavy drawl that evolved somewhere between Brisbane and Alice Springs.

---

* Western Canada often refers to the provinces of British Columbia, Alberta, Saskatchewan, and Manitoba. Since Manitoba and Saskatchewan feature in their own edition, *The Great Canadian Prairies Bucket List*, this book refers only to British Columbia and Alberta.

Regardless of your relationship with the Almighty, we can all understand the Aussie's sentiment, if not always his accent. "God's Country" is an idiom that describes a location of such incredible beauty that it surely belongs in a higher realm.

Having spent twenty years travelling to over one hundred countries on all seven continents, I've found that God's Country has transparent, unlimited borders. Every ecosystem offers a rare beauty. You can drink jungle air like an elixir, hang dreams on the fronds of beach palms, sleep in the desert under a weighted blanket of stars, and inhale unmatched tranquility on the tundra. Yet deep-cut fjords, dense rainforests, soaring snow-tipped mountain peaks, and turquoise glacial lakes are what many a traveller will refer to as the definition of natural beauty. This rustic splendour sits at the very foundation of British Columbia and Alberta — and we're just getting started.

The job and quest of a travel writer is to uncover the remarkable and the unique. We chase destinations and activities, building an intimate knowledge of what sets an experience apart, and how best it can be appreciated. In doing so, we inspire ourselves, and our readers, too. The first edition of this book was published in 2015, extracted from a larger national volume, *The Great Canadian Bucket List*. While I was originally approached to write a guidebook, I felt readers would be better served by storytelling and the emotional draw of each chapter, as opposed to logistical information, which is more current online anyway. It felt to me that we're drowning in *information*, but lacking in *inspiration*. Tracking the spirit bear, sailing in the Galápagos of the North, horseback riding into the Rockies — what does it feel like, who might you meet, what can you learn? If I hoped to write about the best of Western Canada, I had to experience the best of Western Canada. This expanded second edition continues my journey, with dozens of new adventures, beautiful photography, fascinating history, and memorable trivia, all with the goal of inspiring both locals and visitors alike.

Like many new arrivals, my first impression of coastal British Columbia left me speechless. I'd landed in Vancouver as an immigrant without having ever stepped foot in North America before. It was a bright sunny day in August, with spectacular fireworks scheduled that evening in English Bay. The following day, a friend took me to the Gulf Islands. I'd seen fjords and snow-capped mountains in Norway, but the landscape in Scandinavia was not as sweeping, and certainly not as accessible. Later, when I discovered the Canadian Rockies, my previous visits to the Alps and Andes paled in comparison. Yes, you'll find elements of Western Canada's beauty elsewhere, but not on this scale, and certainly not with the region's world-class hotels, dining, transportation, and attractions. B.C. and Alberta's excellent infrastructure and wonderful communities make it exceptionally easy to tick off a bucket list, while inspiring new dreams along the way.

• • •

Beyond the region's natural assets, I sought unique, one-of-a-kind experiences: snorkelling with thousands of salmon, heli-fishing, alpine night skiing, digging for dinosaur fossils, and houseboating, among many others. This new edition also includes a taste of Indigenous experiences, which you can and should engage with in both provinces. There's never been a better time to connect with Indigenous Peoples in Canada, and experience adventure, cuisine, and history through their unique lens.

Since I'd like nothing more than for you to follow in my footsteps, each chapter points to a companion website where you'll find practical information, videos, galleries, and other bonus content.

Admittedly, some of these experiences are not cheap; others, however, are as free as a walk in Stanley Park. There's adventure, food, culture, history — something for everyone. I hope this second volume informs, inspires, and delights readers with my personal journey into Canada's crown jewel. It's been quite the adventure to get it onto these pages, into your hands, and inside your imagination. God's Country is indeed waiting. What are you waiting for?

Disclaimer

Tourism is a constantly evolving industry. Tour operators, restaurants, and hotels often change names or ownership, adapt their services, or cease operations altogether. Records fall, facts shift, and practical information needs to be constantly updated. This is why you'll find a link with each experience to a comprehensive companion website, which contains official links, photo galleries, maps, travel tips, and a blog with bonus experiences too. While the utmost care has been taken to ensure the information provided in this book is accurate, the author and publisher take no responsibility for errors or for any incidents that might occur in your pursuit of these activities.

BRITISH COLUMBIA

DISCOVER HAIDA GWAII

Canada's Galápagos

📍 Gwaii Haanas National Park Reserve, National Marine Conservation
Area Reserve, and Haida Heritage Site
🔗 canadianbucketlist.com/haida

ON BRITISH COLUMBIA'S WEST COAST, BEYOND STORMY
dreams and the knife's edge of the continental shelf, is a 280-kilometre-
long archipelago of unsurpassed myth and scenic beauty. Amid soaring
mountains, crystal-clear creeks, and towering trees, these Pacific islands

are inhabited by a culture whose unique art is instantly recognized, and its language found nowhere else on Earth. When I first set off to discover the best of Canada, I polled fellow travel writers about what tops their own national bucket lists. More often than not, the answer was Haida Gwaii.

Flying into the sleepy village of Sandspit, I catch a ferry to the twenty-six-million-dollar Haida Heritage Site to put our first B.C. adventure in context. Here, I learn about the two Haida clans — Eagles and Ravens — and how they balance each other in marriage, trade, and even death. I learn about the importance of western red cedar, and how imposing totem poles were carved to tell legends, honour men, and identify homesteads. I learn how this proud warrior nation, whose seafaring and ferocity have been compared to that of the Vikings, was all but exterminated after a century of European contact, in a deadly cocktail of disease and cultural genocide. Of the Haida people who thrived on these islands, a staggering 95 percent disappeared. Fortunately, their descendants are staging a remarkable comeback. First, they reclaimed their art, which is recognized worldwide as being among the pinnacle of Indigenous Peoples cultural expression. Next, they reclaimed ownership of their land, in an unprecedented deal with the federal government, so that the former Queen Charlotte Islands became Haida Gwaii (Islands of the People). Now they are relearning and protecting their language, before it, too, becomes a ghost echoing in the forest.

It gives me a lot to think about as Moresby Explorers' four-hundred-horsepower Zodiac speeds down the coast into the vast protected realm of the Gwaii Haanas National Park Reserve, National Marine Conservation Area Reserve, and Haida Heritage Site. I am late for a date with Bluewater Adventures' twenty-one-metre-long Island Roamer, on which I will join a dozen tourists from around the country on a week-long sailing expedition. This 1,470-square-kilometre national park reserve, unique with its stewardship from mountaintop to ocean floor, can only be accessed via boat and float plane. Founded in 1988, the reserve was a hard-fought victory for the Haida against the multinational logging companies that had sheared many islands of their forests. Today, visitor numbers are limited, and respect for the land, sea, and air remains paramount.

I hop on board to meet new friends, engaged with the archipelago's wildlife and beauty and relishing our comfortable yacht to explore it. The two-hundred-plus islands of Gwaii Haanas are dense with old-growth temperate rainforest, boasting forty endemic species of animals and plants while creating a haven for twenty-three types of whale and dozens of seabird species. Sailing the calm waters between the coves and bays of this massive park reserve, we spot humpbacks, seals, sea lions, and a large family of rare offshore orcas.

Bluewater's Zodiac deposits us onshore to explore forests of giant western red cedar, hemlock, and Sitka spruce, the ground carpeted with bright green moss and fern. We walk among the ruins of an old whaling station in Rose Harbour and pick up Japanese garbage on Kunghit Island, blown in with the raging storms of the Pacific. In Echo Harbour, we watch schools of salmon launch themselves from the sea into the creek, and a huge black bear (Haida Gwaii boasts the biggest black bears found anywhere) lick its lips in anticipation. We do the same on the yacht as the chef serves up fresh coconut-crusted halibut and other delights from her small but fully equipped galley.

As an eco-adventure, Gwaii Haanas has a reputation for being "Canada's Galápagos." Having cruised around the Galápagos myself, I found the two experiences share distinct similarities, if not the same landscape or wildlife. Yet it's the legacy of the Haida themselves that elevates this wild, rugged region into true global bucket-list territory, best illustrated by the remarkable UNESCO World Heritage Site of SGang Gwaay. Haida lived here for millennia, but after the plague of

smallpox, European trade, and residential schools, all that remains are eerie carved cedar mortuary poles. Facing the sea like sentinels with the thick forest at their backs, they make it an unforgettable and haunting place to visit, all the more so for the effort it takes to do so. The five Haida village National Historic Sites in Gwaii Haanas — Skedans, Tanu, Windy Bay, Hotspring Island, and SGang Gwaay — are guarded by the Watchmen, local men and women employed by the community and Parks Canada.

James Williams, a Watchman at SGang Gwaay, enthusiastically describes the history of the village and the legacy of the poles. He tells us how the Haida attached supernatural qualities to the animals and trees that surrounded them, hence their culture borne out of tales featuring bears, ravens, eagles, killer whales, otters, and cedar. Unassuming in his baseball cap, James discusses violent battles with mainland tribes, the Haida acumen for trade and canoe building, and their interaction with European sea-otter traders, which ultimately killed off the animal, and very nearly finished off the Haida themselves. Today, these weathered ash-grey mortuary poles are maintained to honour a tradition that once thrived and shows signs of thriving again. Tombstones that seem older than their 150-year-old origins, the poles remind me of the stone heads on Easter Island, or the stone carvings of Angkor in Cambodia. Trees rattle in the onshore breeze as the forest slowly reclaims the remains of abandoned cedar longhouses. James gifts us with some freshly caught halibut as he welcomes some arriving kayakers. With Watchmen having to live in solitude for months at a time, it is not so much a job as a calling.

Each abandoned village is different, and each Watchman reveals more about this rugged west coast wonderland, and the people who call it home. By the end of the week, both the land and its stewards have woven a spell over me. Originally built to last the length of a single lifetime, old Haida totem poles will not stand forever. Fortunately, the protection of Gwaii Haanas, by both the Haida people and Parks Canada, along with the deep respect paid to both by operators like Bluewater Adventures, ensures this magical archipelago will remain on the Western Canada bucket list for generations to come.

HIKE THE WEST COAST TRAIL

Not the hike to break in new boots

⊚ Pacific Rim National Park Reserve
𝒫 canadianbucketlist.com/wct

I'M OVERJOYED THAT I EXPERIENCED THE WEST COAST TRAIL, but happier still that one of the world's great hikes didn't kill me. Hikers come from all over the world to challenge themselves on this rugged seventy-seven-kilometre trail. Shortly after I left the trailhead, I was convinced every one of them must be insane. Case in point: the few wild

BRITISH COLUMBIA

animals you might encounter are those most likely to eat you — bears, wolves, and cougars. The path is treacherous, the weather notorious, and every year about one hundred hikers are evacuated with injuries. Born out of a life-saving trail created alongside the Graveyard of the Pacific, a stretch of coast where more than one thousand ships have run aground, the West Coast Trail is nonetheless a true Canadian challenge, in all its pain and glory.

Snaking up the Pacific Rim National Park Reserve from Bamfield to Port Renfrew, you're far removed from roads, shops, or civilization. That's why park rangers patrol in helicopters and boats looking for wounded hikers suffering from sprains, slips, and hypothermia. Given that fifteen centimetres of rain can fall in just twelve hours, the well-marked trail can quickly become a quagmire of thick mud, sharp rocks, and slippery boardwalks. So why would anyone actually add this to

their bucket list? To find out, I joined a group of seven hikers, allocating our supplies according to our body weights. All our trash would have to be burned or carried out, while lunch would consist only of GORP (granola, oats, raisins, peanuts) and energy bars.

Within the first exhausting hour, evacuation didn't seem like such a bad idea. The rain was holding off, but the path was streaked with tricky roots and knee-deep mud pools. Then came the wooden ladders, some of which climb as high as twenty-five metres. With my knees creaking under the weight of my twenty-five-kilogram backpack, I stumble into camp seven hours later, collapsing in a heap.

"The nice thing about hurting your ankle is you forget how much your back and feet hurt," says my friend Andrew, dealing with a sprained

THE BEST MULTIDAY HIKES IN WESTERN CANADA

Between the mountains, forests, lakes, and Pacific Ocean, Western Canada is blessed with incredible multiday, pack-in hikes. Here are some of the best:

Skyline Trail, Alberta: Kicking off at Maligne Lake in Jasper National Park, expect jaw-dropping panoramic views of the Rockies, mountain wildlife, creek crossings, and quality time above the treeline on this popular forty-four-kilometre-long trail.

Berg Lake Trail, B.C.: Located in Mount Robson Provincial Park, brace yourself for three thousand metres of ascent in this forty-two-kilometre round-trip hike to magnificent Berg Lake, where you can camp on the shoreline listening to calving glaciers.

Juan de Fuca Trail, B.C.: Often mentioned alongside the West Coast Trail, this challenging forty-seven-kilometre coastal hike on Vancouver Island also features sandy beaches, rainforests, ladders, cable cars, ocean views, and unpredictable weather.

Tonquin Valley Trail, Alberta: Another Jasper National Park highlight, this forty-four-kilometre loop Great Divide Trail between B.C. and Alberta packs in the mountain views.

Rockwall Trail, B.C.: Traversing three major passes in Kootenay National Park, this fifty-four-kilometre trail traces an imposing limestone cliff, with alpine lakes, imposing glaciers, waterfalls, and backcountry wildlife.

Tamarack Trail, Alberta: This thirty-two-kilometre, two-day hike is one of the most popular trails in Waterton Lakes National Park, and it's particularly spectacular in late September and early October, when the namesake tamarack trees explode with fall colours.

Chilkoot Trail, B.C.: Steeped in gold rush history, follow the rugged trail of nineteenth-century speculators in this fifty-three-kilometre trail between Alaska and B.C. The terrain is steep, the weather unpredictable, and the experience priceless.

Northover Ridge, Alberta: A thirty-six-kilometre loop located in Kananaskis's Peter Lougheed Provincial Park, this challenging hike straddles the continental divide with a narrow high alpine ridge, a 1,500-metre elevation gain, and the epic reward of rugged mountain adventure.

Mount Assiniboine Provincial Park, B.C.: Located south of Banff but still in B.C., the "Matterhorn of the Rockies" has various multiday hikes, ranging from forty-two to sixty kilometres return.

ankle and receiving absolutely no sympathy. Each hiker's pain is their own. The key to success, according to Kyle, our veteran leader with several West Coast Trails under his belt, is preparation. We have all the essentials: walking sticks, gaiters, camel packs, dehydrated food, good tents, a water pump.

"Inexperienced hikers are usually the first to go," a park ranger had told me earlier. "This is not the trail to break in new boots."

We build our campfires beside driftwood benches and bathe in freezing streams. All food is locked in communal bear lockers overnight, and one morning we awake to find fresh wolf prints beside our tents, just in case we'd thought we were alone. Halfway into the week-long hike, my pack begins to lighten and my muscles harden. I stop kvetching long enough to admire the massive Douglas-fir trees, the sea arches, limestone cliffs, waterfalls, sandy beaches, and crystal tidal pools bristling with luminous purple starfish and green anemones. The camaraderie with fellow hikers from around the world, met along the way or in camp, tops up this natural inspiration. Sharing tips on what to expect up ahead, we're all pushing our mental and physical limits. Each day we hike between eleven and seventeen kilometres of challenging terrain.

At the end of the week, food consumed and camera batteries low, I trudge along the final twelve kilometres to the end, grateful for a few extra-strength painkillers. Our group is haggard, dirty, sore — and utterly elated. "Few finish this adventure pain-free," reads a popular hiking website. Why is the West Coast Trail on the bucket list? For the challenge, the beauty, the communal spirit, and the opportunity to say, "Yes, I did it, and it didn't kill me!"

SNOWMOBILE IN THE KOOTS

An ambush of winter adventure

⦿ Invermere
🔗 canadianbucketlist.com/koots

I'M HAVING DINNER WITH AN AMERICAN WRITER, A FIRST-TIME visitor to Canada. Picking away at her introductory plate of poutine, we're discussing the cultural differences that span the forty-ninth parallel. In the United States, I explain, incredible natural attractions are usually heavily marketed. In Canada, I'll often explore a destination

18

or region, and a guide or local will just modestly mention that there's something worth seeing. No signposts, no gift shops. When I inevitably show up at that something, it kicks me hard in the bucket list.

We're in the Kootenays, a mountainous region in southeastern British Columbia, famed for its abundant natural beauty and incredible all-season outdoor recreation. Originally dependant on forestry and mining, the region offers three exceptional national parks, an alluring quality of life, and some of the best skiing anywhere. We had already explored the vibrant mountain towns of Fernie and Kimberley, with time well spent on the slopes at their fantastic namesake ski resorts. Fernie's craft beer, local distillery, and Big Bang Bagels make it well worth the stop, as does dining along Kimberley's Bavarian-inspired Platzl, overlooked by the world's largest standing — and inexplicably yodelling — cuckoo clock. It's great stuff, but doesn't quite prove my thesis about shoulder-shrugging, no-big-deal local Canadian attractions ambushing the imagination. For that, we'll have to hop on snowmobiles.

Let's raise a toast to Joseph-Armand Bombardier, the Quebecois mechanic who built the world's first snowmobile back in 1935. The machines are easy and fun to ride, open up a world of winter possibilities, and allow us to effortlessly ride up a steep mountain track almost 2,500 metres above sea level to an abandoned silver mine. Toby Creek Adventures, located opposite the Panorama Mountain Resort outside of Invermere, owns this sweeping alpine terrain, with tenure for nearly thirty-five thousand acres more. As with zip-lining, any snowmobile adventure tends to be as special as the location in which you do it, and Toby Creek's Paradise Ridge and Basin is about as special as it gets. I stop to ogle the ski slopes streaking down Panorama Mountain, the apex of Mount Goldie, and the rocky crest of Mount Nelson. We have heated handles on our snowmobiles, ample power, and friendly guides to help navigate the switchbacks. Both first-time and veteran riders are elated when we pause for hot chocolate inside a heated log cabin.

With the blessing of our guides, we let the snowmobiles loose in Paradise Basin, revving the engines over the hills and bending into the curves. Great stuff yet again, but the true, jaw-dropping, OMG-caps-locked-ONLY-IN-CANADA moment finally presents itself on our descent into the valley. I know it's coming, because our guide pulls over, and he casually asks us if we want to see a frozen waterfall. Just a short walk through the trees, he tells us, you know, a little attraction worth checking out. If you've seen one frozen waterfall, you've seen them … no. Trust me, you have not seen Marmot Falls.

SKATE WITH THE WINDERMERE AT YOUR BACK

The world's longest skating path is on Lake Windermere in Invermere, B.C. Every year, the Toby Creek Nordic Ski Club grooms a thirty-kilometre-plus track around this gorgeous lake, adding cross-country skiing and fat-biking trails, and curling and hockey rinks for good measure. Framed by the Rockies and the Purcell Mountain range, the path has two main access points, with entrance by donation to support the multi-use path's impressive maintenance. As a non-skater myself, I was quite happy to walk along the path, spotting ice-fishing cabins in the distance and bubbles suspended in ice beneath my feet. Ambitious (and very fit) skaters might want to take on the whole path, or loop back somewhere along the way.

It looks like a frost giant has frozen a raging cascade in mid-motion. Named after squirrelly rodents chittering in the trees around us, the winter spectacle of Marmot Falls is the result of ice forming at the top and bottom of the waterfall, eventually meeting in the middle to expand outward. It's the colour that hits you first — a deep glacial blue, contrasted by the late afternoon sky and powder white snow. Icy torrents somehow appear to flow downward. I find myself rubbing my eyes, clearing away any doubt that I'm actually here, that this is actually happening, and I'm not lapsing into the kind of dream you have when your young daughter watches *Frozen* for the thirty-ninth time. "Does anybody want to slide down?" asks our guide. A channel has been carved in the ice, creating a slide long enough to generate a thrill, and a photograph worth printing for posterity.

Here it is, I tell my American friend. "Another perfect example of a unique, little-known attraction that epitomizes the wonders of Western Canada." Marmot Falls could, and one day might, feature on a billboard, but the Kootenays are too rugged, glorious, and free for tour buses.

DIVE A SUNKEN BATTLESHIP

Big things in cold water

📍 Nanaimo
🔗 canadianbucketlist.com/scuba

WITH THE PRESS OF A BUTTON, I DESCEND INTO THE COLD, DARK murk of the Pacific. It's a far cry from the warm turquoise waters of Papua New Guinea, where I learned to scuba dive. Yet the coast of Vancouver Island is renowned for its diving, with the late Jacques Cousteau rating B.C. the second-best temperate dive spot in the world, behind the Red Sea.

To see for myself, I'll have to adapt. At these temperatures, dry suits are necessary, allowing divers to remain warm in an airtight bubble. This kind of diving also requires extra training, so I've called on Greg McCracken, one of B.C.'s top instructors, to introduce me to the province's submersible wonders.

Greg has picked out one of the most spectacular dives on offer: exploring the sunken destroyer HMCS *Saskatchewan*, which sits upright on the ocean floor not far from the ferry port of Vancouver Island's Departure Bay. The Artificial Reef Society of British Columbia is a world leader in creating environmentally protective reefs, having sunk seven warships and one Boeing 737 in local waters to attract indigenous marine life, creating sustainable, attractive diving destinations.

• • •

It's a crisp morning when Sea Dragon Charters' dive boat anchors to a buoy alongside Snake Island, home to 250 harbour seals. Though the water is a brisk 7°C, my dry suit is insulated and comfortable. After descending twenty metres, we see the first anemones, rocking in the ocean currents. A huge lingcod is perfectly camouflaged against the reef, which I soon realize is, in fact, metal, part of the 111-metre-long Mackenzie-class destroyer. Our flippers propel us forward, and I see the old cannons, now exploding with life. There are huge spiky copper rockfish, purple California sea cucumbers, assorted sculpins, and thousands of dancing brittle stars. Since this ship was sunk in 1997, marine life has gladly taken the place of the 230 officers who once lived aboard.

We descend to twenty-nine metres before making our way back up. After making the required safety stops to avoid decompression sickness, we climb aboard the boat, elated. "The size and abundance of marine life in B.C. really sets it apart," explains Greg over hot chocolate. "You

BRITISH COLUMBIA'S TOP DIVES

Greg and Deirdre McCracken, owners of B.C.'s Ocean Quest Dive Centre and two of the province's most respected divers, list their Top 10:

1. Browning Wall (boat dive) — Port Hardy
2. Skookumchuck Rapids (boat dive) — Egmont
3. Steep Island (boat dive) — Campbell River
4. Renate Reef (boat dive) — Barkley Sound
5. Dodd Narrows (boat dive) — Nanaimo
6. Race Rocks (boat dive) — Victoria
7. HMCS *Saskatchewan* (boat dive) — Nanaimo
8. Wreck of the *Capilano* (boat dive) — Comox
9. Whytecliff Park (shore dive) — Vancouver
10. Ogden Point (shore dive) — Victoria

experience things underwater here that you just can't experience anywhere else."

Just a few hundred feet away is another artificial wreck, one of the world's largest upright reefs and one of B.C.'s most popular diving locations. The HMCS *Cape Breton* is a 134-metre-long Second World War Victory ship, built for action in 1944, converted into an escort and maintenance ship soon after, and ultimately sunk upright onto a flat seabed off Snake Island in 2001. We suit up again, check our air pressure, add weights to our belts. The massive *Cape Breton* cannot be explored in one dive. I feel like a small bird exploring a double-decker bus. I follow Greg through a long corridor, peering with my flashlight into various rooms, noticing the fish, plants, and sponges that have moved in. We hover over the engine room skylights, but Greg has warned me that it's only for technical, well-trained divers. When you're thirty metres underwater, connected to life by an oxygen tank, it's best not to argue.

Note: Diving should only be attempted with the proper training, available across the country. If you have ear problems, as I do, look into Doc's Proplugs — they're worth their weight in underwater treasure.

HIT THE SURF

> Less ego, more wilderness

📍 Tofino
🔗 canadianbucketlist.com/tofino

CANADA MAY BE A COLD NORTHERN COUNTRY, BUT Canadians can still live for the surf, philosophize about the rhythm of the ocean, and call each other "dude." Tofino is not Malibu or Haleiwa, but then Vancouver Island is not California or Hawaii. This laid-back yet booming surf town demands a commitment to the waves, not

SURF'S UP

After renting your gear and taking a lesson with one of Tofino's surf schools, head to one of these popular surf spots:

Cox Bay: One and a half kilometres long, it's the most consistent break in the area, and probably the most popular surf destination in the country.

Florencia Bay: Five kilometres long, facing mostly south, this is one of the quieter beaches, with a steep shoreline offering protection from cold westerly winds.

Chesterman Beach: Popular with locals and families, Chesterman has forgiving swells for the best beginner breaks in Tofino.

Wickaninnish Beach: Located at the south end of the sixteen-kilometre, aptly named Long Beach, Wickaninnish faces west with an epic coastline.

sun-bleached hair and bikinis. When you surf in a full-body wetsuit, all hipness dissipates.

Tofino sits on the wild west coast of Vancouver Island, battered by volatile weather that washes up debris along its long sandy beaches, shredding trees in the surrounding Pacific Rim National Park Reserve. Storm-watching is a popular pastime in the spring and fall, best enjoyed from the large picture windows of the Wickaninnish Inn, one of the finest hotels in the country. Tofino offers whale watching, hot springs, fantastic restaurants, and contemplative hikes in old-growth forest. For Canadians embracing surf culture, there's no better place to be. Although the climate can be extreme, the surf community is unusually friendly. Visitors from southern surf towns enjoy the fact that territorial testosterone is kept to a minimum.

Guided by instructors from Surf Sister, one of the most popular surf schools in town, I enter the 10°C water insulated from head to toe. Although waves can reach up to ten metres, today they're providing a gentle introduction to the art of riding them. Just several metres into the waters of Cox Bay, I sit on my board and admire the unkempt beach cradled by a wind-battered forest. There are no bars, clothing stores, or

A GROOVY BIKE-THROUGH LOBBY

Hotel Zed's bright angular pinks, purples, and oranges glow like a lava lamp amidst the dense forest outside of Tofino. The uniquely fun seventies-themed hotel — complete with a lime green shag carpet in the sunken lounge, dial phones, knitted macramé, and other elements steeped in nostalgia — has North America's first bike-through lobby. The six-kilometre-long multi-use bike path that runs along the highway from Tofino to the popular beaches takes a brightly painted detour directly into the lobby of Hotel Zed. Automatic doors encourage guests and visitors to cycle through, waving to staff and guests along the way.

hard bodies glistening in the sun. Instead of birds in bikinis, bald eagles soar overhead. It's my first time on a surfboard, and while the waves may be timid, I still spend the afternoon wiping out, falling off my long board with the grace of a flying ostrich. When I do stand up, for just a moment, the heavens sing hallelujah, and an eagle swoops by to give me a congratulatory wink. Maybe I've swallowed too much of the Pacific and I'm not thinking straight. What does it matter? Without attitude or pushiness, ego or tan lines, surfing the wilderness of Vancouver Island keeps your soul warm just as surely as a wetsuit. Even if you don't manage to get up.

HOUSEBOAT ON SHUSWAP LAKE

Portable glamping, on the water and under the stars

📍 Sicamous

🔗 canadianbucketlist.com/shuswap

IT'S MY FIRST TIME CAPTAINING ANY MARINE VESSEL, NEVER mind a twenty-metre-long, five-metre-high floating house with a hot tub, fireplace, washer-dryer, and waterslide. Having already sat through an orientation video, I listen closely as friendly Sicamous Houseboats staff walk me through the *Queen's Crown*. After my fellow passengers

load our luggage into the seven staterooms, I grip the ship wheel to navigate a narrow marina channel, making sure to keep inbound boats on my left. The engine revving low, we putter beneath two road and rail bridges, then I cautiously point the vessel north, edging her throttle forward as we cruise into one of Canada's very best outdoor experiences.

The eighty-nine-kilometre-long Shuswap Lake branches into four distinct arms, framed by forest, mountains, and beaches. A sparkling freshwater paradise that's rightly known as the Houseboating Capital of Canada, it offers a compelling proposition: up to two dozen of your closest friends and family members can enjoy stellar scenery and silky warm water, bringing home comforts — hot showers, flush toilets, a fully equipped kitchen, Weber BBQs, double beds, a lounge, and a dining room — with you. It's portable glamping, on the water and under the stars.

An hour before sunset, all houseboats must beach for the night, and there's no shortage of sandy or pebble beach to accommodate. Wild houseboat celebrations are legendary on the Shuswap, if that's what you're into. All summer, bachelor, bachelorette, and other parties congregate on Nielsen Beach, where many a damage deposit has been lost. With my extended family on board, including kids, parents, cousins, and close friends, my party days have long since sailed. Cold beer and fine wine will still flow, but we're here to relax. Luckily, Shuswap Lake has over one thousand kilometres of shoreline, encompassing nearly two dozen provincial parks. There's ample space for everybody.

I turn the engine off so everyone can enjoy the waterslide and bust out their floaties in the deep, clean, and warm fresh water. As the sun descends, we beach the vessel and prepare dinner while the teenagers on board search in vain for cellphone service. Grilling up wild sockeye — something taken for granted in this part of the world — we build a beach fire for s'mores and then hot tub under the stars.

Sicamous Houseboats' thirty boats are fully equipped, comfortable, and spotless. All you need to bring are clothes, bedding, food, towels, deck chairs, coolers, and flashlights. The *Queen's Crown* is a two-deck Mirage 65 vessel that sleeps eighteen passengers in beds (doubled up) and four more in the living room. The Genesis 66 has three decks and a twirly waterslide, while the Mirage 40 is suited for smaller families. Shuswap Lake is renowned as a motorboat mecca, but the wakeboards, Jet Skis, and speedboats thin out as we cruise north to explore the best hike in the region: the five-kilometre loop trail to Albas Falls. Locals had told me this was the best spot on the lake, and they were right. We easily access the trailhead for a two-hour hike to a series of five gorgeous cascades. If you're going to do one hike, this is it.

I do wonder how our experience might differ with strong winds, heavy rain, or choppy waves. But it's early September and the weather

gods are smiling. With a recent lifting of a campfire ban, the magic of B.C.'s outdoors is ours to plunder.

By our 10:00 a.m. checkout time on our final day, I'm surprised how comfortable I've become at the wheel, the basics now ingrained. Anyone over twenty-five years old with a driver's licence can captain the boat, and sharing the duties with my co-captains allowed plenty of time to relax.

While mishaps do happen — especially on the party boats — Sicamous Houseboats' owner Barb Scott tells me that most clients take great care with the boats, and the hefty five-thousand-dollar damage deposit takes care of the rest. Yes, between the boat rental and fuel costs, high season on the Mirage 60 can run over two thousand dollars a night. This is not cheap, but glamping rarely is, and you can split the cost among multiple families or a dozen friends.

Immersed in spectacular nature, wrapped in physical comforts, surrounded by family and friends, and relishing an adventure of a lifetime — what more could anyone ask for? Despite an early round of nerves, my first houseboat getaway resulted in a very happy captain, with a solid tick cruising on his bucket list.

TRACK THE SPIRIT BEAR

Legends in the Great Bear Rainforest

⚲ Gribbell Island
🔗 canadianbucketlist.com/spiritbear

PACIFIC COASTAL AIRLINES' AMPHIBIOUS GRUMMAN GOOSE splashes down, and clearly the Great Bear Rainforest is in good spirits. Absent on this fine mid-September afternoon is the notorious west coast weather, replaced by a beaming sun striking the Pacific Ocean like a spotlight on a mirror ball. What's more, the familiar face I'd seen at the Vancouver airport is along for the ride, a man who knows this area better than most: David Suzuki, Canada's most respected environmentalist.

We have come to explore this unspoiled temperate rainforest, stretching sixty-four thousand square kilometres from northern B.C. to the Alaska border. It encompasses hundreds of islands, dozens of First Nations communities, vast amounts of wildlife, and one peculiar animal that has long captured the public imagination: a bear with a coat as white as snow, roaming the forest creeks like a mist in search of substance. Fewer than one thousand are said to exist, with a spirit so powerful they have never been hunted. A recessive gene gives the rare Kermode bear, commonly known as the spirit bear, its distinctive white coat. Not an albino, not a different species, just a family of black rainforest bears that pass on an unusual trait, like a tribe of redheads living in the Amazon.

We settle into a cozy fishing lodge, ready for the adventure. Some of us hope to hook giant halibut, or hike into the mountains among the old-growth trees. Others want to see the hundreds of humpbacks, orca, and fin whales that feed in the rich sea channels. We can also visit the Gitga'at, our closest First Nations community, to meet elders and learn about their fascinating culture in Hartley Bay. But the star attraction at this time of year, when millions of salmon begin their final journey up the creeks, are the great bears that give the region its name, coming out to feast.

After an hour-long boat ride along the tidal zone of Princess Royal Island, we dock across the channel on Gribbell Island, and are greeted by a man who has lived and worked with the spirit bears his entire life. Marven Robinson is the go-to guy for the Kermode, the man who introduces film crews, tourists, and journalists to this magical animal. Marven personally constructed wooden platforms along Riordan Creek in places that least disturb the bears but allow visitors to observe them in their natural habitat. "I'm here to protect the bears," he says, "not the people."

Supplied with sandwiches and hot soup, we begin the wait. Marven discusses his passion for protecting the bears and the land they live in. David Suzuki tells me about the fight to save the region from becoming an oil supertanker highway, and how, despite huge financial incentives, the First Nations have joined conservationists to say enough is enough. Below us, hundreds of pink salmon are spawning, squirming, darting upstream. It's this abundance of food that will draw the bears, eventually. We talk *sotto voce*, swatting bugs from our faces.

Finally, there's a ripple of excitement. A large black bear is making its way downstream. It stops, swipes a mouthful of salmon from a pool, and tears it to pieces. Slowly, the bear ambles along the river, stopping right beneath our platform, oblivious to our quiet presence. I hear the sound of memory cards filling up, and then an excited whisper: "There it is!"

A large Kermode male, all 135 kilos of him, six years old by Marven's reckoning, is approaching. Ethereal, pink-nosed, with cream-white fur at odds with the earthy tones of its surroundings, the Kermode chases salmon, spraying water drops that reflect the early afternoon sunlight. Suddenly the black bear charges aggressively, sending the Kermode up a mossy bank. Unperturbed, it re enters a few metres downstream and continues its hunt for, as I'm told, as many as eighty fish a day. Finally, both bears wander off, leaving us spellbound. There's no guarantee you'll see the spirit bear on any given day, and more than once on my journey I've found myself facing the wrong end of the barrel of fortune. But not today.

The First Nations have always protected the spirit bear, believing it has a powerful effect on all who are lucky enough to see it. My own encounter left me deeply inspired by the Great Bear Rainforest, along with the creatures that inhabit, protect, and nurture its future — the Gitga'at, Marven Robinson, and David Suzuki ... and the spirit bear, which radiates magic and brings it all together.

SNORKEL WITH SALMON

Eye to eye with B.C.'s most influential fish

⦿ Campbell River
🔗 canadianbucketlist.com/salmon

NEXT TIME YOU ORDER SUSHI, SPARE A THOUGHT FOR THE miracle of Canada's Pacific salmon. Half a billion of them, returning from a five-thousand-kilometre journey in the open ocean, spawn in the very gravel, in the very river, where they themselves once hatched. In the process, they must survive the appetites of seals, sharks, eagles, sea

THE SOCKEYE RUN ON THE ADAMS RIVER

If you prefer to stay dry but still want a bucket-list salmon experience, head to the Adams River, located about a one-hour drive from Kamloops. Each Thanksgiving, as many as 250,000 people visit the Salute to the Sockeye Festival to see the world's largest return of sockeye salmon to a single river, especially during a dominant run every four years. To see the fish clearly, polarized sunglasses are a must, and there's plenty of space to observe the salmon in motion. Enjoy the migration of people, drawn to the migration of a species that people love to eat.

lions, bears, and of course humans. Leaping from pond to pond, battling predators, starvation, suffocation, overcrowding, and fierce interspecies competition, their backs hump, their noses hook, and their skin turns bright red as finally they are ready to mate. Having accomplished this extraordinary feat of derring-do, the salmon, unlike their Atlantic cousins, promptly die. Why these kamikaze pilots are drawn to B.C.'s rivers is still something of a mystery, but it certainly has something to do with the abundance of fresh water, filtered by the temperate rainforest. As the spent bodies of salmon wash downstream, they continue to feed up to two hundred species in the forest. Some 80 percent of the nitrogen in forest soil can be traced to salmon, nitrogen that's vital for hemlock, spruce, and cedar to grow. Delicious as they may be (smoked, barbecued, fried, or grilled), there simply wouldn't be a B.C. without its annual salmon run — which you can witness first-hand, underwater, in Campbell River.

Renting a full-body wetsuit, snorkel, and fins from a local dive shop, I'm directed to an ideal entry spot at the logging bridge on the Gold

BRITISH COLUMBIA

River Highway. A hydroelectric project regulates the river's water supply, making it a particularly fun place to do what I'm about to do. Which is: hop in the water, point my body downriver, float with the current, and immerse myself in this little-seen world of salmon — hundreds of thousands of them.

Five different species of salmon migrate through these waters: Chinook, chum, sockeye, coho, and pink. I will mostly be seeing pink salmon today, interspersed with giant Chinooks, along with opportunist rainbow and steelhead trout (yet another predator for nature's ultimate survivors). This enormous bounty of fish means I won't be alone. Locals line the riverbanks with their rods, catching their seasonal quota, or catch-and-releasing in hopes of hooking a true beast: a mighty thirty-two-kilogram Chinook was caught in the area in 2010. Locals watch snorkellers each summer with a mix of curiosity and envy, for once we enter the brisk current of the river, we can see exactly where the fish are. And wow, they are everywhere.

Wetsuits suitably disarm the 10°C water as I enter the river. From above, I had seen streaks of grey darting in the green-brown water. Underwater, there are salmon everywhere — walls of them, floors of them, cities and towns and planets of them. Despite the obstacles that began the moment they were born, in just one corner I see enough survivors to assuage a feeling of guilt. Certain stocks are threatened, and the debate over farmed salmon versus wild rages on, but today there seems to be a fish for every Tom, Dick, and hungry Harry.

The current carries me into more schools with a sensation that is part buoyancy, part flying. For a moment I feel like a fish myself, nervously watching for rocks, large predators, and deceptive bait. Most of all, though, I'm just having fun, in awe of a fish that shaped the environment of the west coast, and that, against all the odds, finds itself on *The Great Western Canada Bucket List*.

GO CAT- OR HELI-SKIING

Either way, you win

📍 Smithers and Nakusp

🔗 canadianbucketlist.com/catvsheli

WELCOME TO A WORLD OF DEEP POWDER, UNTOUCHED RUNS, and epic mountain terrain. There are no ski chairs or busy lineups, in fact there are no crowds whatsoever. No grading or crunchy corduroy, no out-of-bounds ropes, no shopping strips, hotels, or parking lots. This is a world measured in vertical feet. It's not a cheap world to visit, because you're going to need the specialized services of a modified helicopter or PistenBully snow groomer. Cat-skiing and heli-skiing etch virgin lines directly onto the trophy case of any skier or snowboarder's bucket list. So, how do they stack up against each other?

B.C.'S BEST HELI- AND CAT-SKI OPERATIONS

Spanning diverse terrain, accommodation, logistics, and guide personalities, there are no losers in this list of top B.C. ski operations:

Heli-Skiing

1. Northern Escape Heli Skiing (Terrace)
2. CMH (eleven lodges across the B.C. interior)
3. Bella Coola Heli Sports (five lodges, Bella Coola/ Anahim Lake)
4. Skeena Heliskiing (Smithers)
5. RK. Heliski (Panorama Mountain Resort)
6. Silvertip Lodge & Heli-Skiing (Williams Lake)

Cat-Skiing

1. Skeena Cat Skiing (Smithers)
2. Keefer Lake Lodge (Kelowna)
3. Big Red Cats (RED Mountain Ski Resort, Rossland)
4. Monashee Powder Snowcats (Cherryville)
5. Mustang Powder (Revelstoke)
6. Great Northern Snowcat Skiing (Trout Lake)

Cat-skiing puts you inside a heated cabin attached to a snow groomer with the torque and tread of an indestructible tank. The driver ascends white-knuckle inclines, skirting dramatic ridges and cornices, and deposits you at the top of seventh heaven – not the famous ski lift in Whistler, but the *real* seventh heaven — over and over again. To sample this experience, I travelled to Skeena Cat Skiing's base camp, accessed via an exhilarating helicopter ride from the town of Smithers. Buried in snow, it looked like an alien settlement on an ice planet. Guests stay in comfortably heated dome tents and gather in the adjacent lounge to drink craft beer, feast on great meals, and unpack the day's events. Typically, that will have consisted of a dozen runs, covering about fifteen thousand vertical feet, and unabashed "can-it-get-any-better" skiing.

Safety is taken very seriously, but don't let the risks — which exist with backcountry *anything* — stop you. You don't want to miss out on those moments where snow and ski and body and mind converge into an unforgettable peak experience.

Think about the best ski run you've *ever* had at a ski resort. Now concentrate that feeling, increase the elation at least tenfold, and you'll get a sense of what it's like to cat-ski in this part of the world. Meeting the Cat at the bottom of a gulley, my group climbs aboard, whooping and hollering, discussing the lines and glades and bowls. The Cat shifts into gear, treads bite into the snow, and here we go. By the end of the day, my legs are exhausted. Cat-skiing, wherever you happen to do it, never gets tired for a second.

Heli-skiing has long been regarded as the apex experience in alpine recreational sport. It will take you higher, faster, wilder, and deeper than any other mountain activity. For this one, I entered the world of CMH Heli-Skiing, who operate almost a dozen immaculate ski lodges across the Columbia Mountain ranges of B.C. It took a couple days for my legs and technique to adjust to powder this thick, and for my brain to compute that a large whirlybird can function as a personal ski chair. Helicopters are pricey to operate, and heli-skiing in B.C. is no cheap endeavour. It typically attracts guests from around the world, pampered in remote, wood-beamed luxury lodges that treat high-end clientele the way high-end clientele like to be treated.

Skiers might average twenty-five to thirty thousand vertical feet each day, with access to millions of acres of terrain. This works out to between eight and twelve runs a day, and you're going to need every run you can get to acclimatize to the powder and daily lifestyle. Early morning yoga classes were essential to stretch tired muscles into shape. Avalanche safety is taken seriously, everyone is well-equipped, and the expert guides know this terrain well. The Canadian heli-ski industry is well regulated, and avalanche incidents are extremely rare. By the third day, when I at last find my footing, I scream with joy, grateful for the opportunity to live on a planet where something like this is even a possibility. Heli-skiing is elation distilled, and the very peak of winter adventure.

The pros and cons? Cat-skiing is cheaper than heli-skiing, but you won't get as high in the peaks, and your runs will be shorter. Heli-skiing is more intense: load in quick, exit quick, go go go! Cat-skiing can run in all weather, while entire heli-days can be scrapped because of storms, poor visibility, or strong winds. The pace of heli-skiing means that social interaction is mostly limited to après at the lodge, while cat-skiing gathers everyone after each run for excitable chatter. Both pack lunches on the go. Skeena Cat's lodge is a family affair; you meet the owners, play with their bear-sized dog, and use the honour-system bar. CMH lodges are well-run mountain hotels, with hot tubs and a fine wine list. The bad news, it has to be said, is that both cat-skiing and heli-skiing will forever change the way you experience resort skiing. No matter how good your day is on the slopes of Whistler or Lake Louise, Vale, Aspen, or the Alps, it will never match the thrill of a cat or heli. Comparing them is not quite apples to apples, but more like champagne to prosecco. Who wins in the meaningless debate of cat-skiing vs. heli-skiing? The answer is simple: you.

SURVIVE THE COLD CHAMBER

A spa to freeze into memory

⚲ Sparkling Hill Resort, Vernon
⃝ canadianbucketlist.com/coldsauna

YOU, TOO, CAN ENJOY THE HEALTH BENEFITS OF FREEZING TO death. And benefits there must be, otherwise guests wouldn't pay for what they're paying for at Sparkling Hill, a fetching, Austrian-style resort located near the interior town of Vernon. Owned by the Swarovski family and adorned with over ten million dollars worth of their crystals,

WESTERN CANADA'S BEST SPAS

Fairmont Spa Banff Springs (Banff): Located inside the iconic mountain resort, this highly rated spa offers a range of treatments, including massages, facials, scrubs, hydrotherapy, a mineral pool, eucalyptus steam, and outdoor hot tubs.

Scandinave Spa (Whistler): Shh ... this quiet, meditative spa has a range of Scandinavian-inspired treatments, with thermal therapy, steams, solariums, Swedish massages, and a range of pools and saunas.

Pacific Mist Spa and Hydropath at the Kingfisher Resort (Courtenay): Expect top-notch massages, facials, and various indoor and outdoor pools, as well as the eight unique elements of the Hydropath including the Steam Cave, Glacial Waterfall, and Sea Mineral Soak.

Kananaskis Nordic Spa (Kananaskis Village): An adult-only, cellphone-free zone of tranquility set in the Rockies, this spa features a range of hot and cold pools, saunas, steam rooms, massages, facials, and other treatments.

Ancient Cedars Spa at Wickaninnish Inn (Tofino): The finest hotel on the beach has a range of spa treatments, including massages, body treatments, and facials. It features a hot tub, steam room, and relaxation lounge with views of the rugged Pacific.

Chi, the Spa at the Shangri-La Hotel (Vancouver): In addition to massages and body treatments, Chi offers a range of "journeys," including a Clarity Ritual in a relaxing Lola Apothecary Rose Milk bath, the half-day Alchemist's Retreat, and The Serenity's flower nectar bath.

Grotto Spa at Tigh-Na-Mara (Parksville): This spa is known for a unique mineral pool that replicates the experience of bathing in a natural hot spring. It also offers a variety of treatments, including massages, facials, and body wraps.

Sparkling Hill has an ambience that is steeped in old world luxury, even with its modern crystal fireplaces, stunning pools, and themed steam rooms in the award-winning KurSpa. I'm wooing my wife with these facts in the four seconds before her panic attack sets in. To be fair, we are wearing bathing suits in a small room whose temperature is a frosty −60°C. Sorry, that's the second room; her real panic attack hits in the third room, which is nearly twice as cold. Hey, she's Brazilian, they freeze to death quicker than the rest of us.

A visit to North America's first (and at time of writing, only) Cryo Cold Chamber provides a treatment in something called cryotherapy, which activates biochemical, hormonal, and immune processes to give your circulatory and nervous systems a healthy kick-start. Sports stars apparently swear by it, whereas I was just swearing, intensely, under my breath, while my eyelashes froze and my nasal passages turned into a glacier. Strictly monitored, my wife and I are told to wear bathing suits, supplemented with gloves and slippers. In order to prevent any humidity that might freeze you in your tracks, we enter the cold sauna through three separate rooms: the first a balmy −15°C, the second −60°C, and the final corker −110°C. Here we must walk in small circles for three long minutes, encouraged by a bundled-up spa worker. Ever jump into a freezing cold lake? Multiply the shock by fifty, and go ahead and punch yourself in the throat for good measure. My wife understandably freaks out, and the spa worker quickly ushers her out to safety. Meanwhile, I continue walking with three elderly ladies in a tight circle, all of us trying not to touch each other in case we fuse.

Bob Marley is blasting from in-chamber speakers, stirring up mental images of frozen corpses washing up on the beach. As I twitch with cold, icicle nipples ready to break off, my testicles having retreated deep into my pancreas, the three minutes come to an end and we rush out of the chamber. Time may fly when you're having fun, but when you're

freezing to death, a single Bob Marley song is like an infant reciting *War and Peace*. Here's the best part: once you exit the cold sauna, you're not allowed to hop in a hot tub or steam room. I assume it's because the rush of blood would explode your head like a champagne cork. Rather, we are told to rest in our robes and drink a warm cup of tea.

The spa suggests you need multiple treatments (sold in blocks of ten) for the cryotherapy to be effective — flash-freezing muscle inflammation, improving joint and muscle function, and relieving skin irritation — although one visit was perfectly adequate for my purposes. My wife did (eventually) forgive me, and once again I learned that what doesn't kill you only makes you appreciate the bizarre things people pay good money for.

EXPLORE AN OLD-GROWTH FOREST

⚑ Port Renfrew
🔗 canadianbucketlist.com/oldgrowth

YES, THEY'RE JUST TREES, KIDS, BUT LOOK AT THE SIZE OF them! The red cedars, Douglas firs, hemlocks, and spruces that survive in the old-growth forests of British Columbia are awesome to behold. Somehow, these giants survived the colonial building boom and modern logging industry, and today they range in age between 250 and

over 1,000 years old. Standing between 800-year-old Douglas-fir trees — towering up to seventy-five metres high in Cathedral Grove inside Vancouver Island's MacMillan Provincial Park — you can't help but feel you're on another planet. The forest moon of Endor comes to mind, although I'm dating myself with *Star Wars*.

Perhaps the kids will prefer Avatar Grove, fifteen minutes away from Port Renfrew, so nicknamed for this ancient red cedar and Douglas fir forest's resemblance to the planet Pandora in the blockbuster *Avatar*. Surrounded by a drapery of ferns and moss, with a soundtrack of chattering woodpeckers or bubbling brooks, I expect a spell of peace and wonder will envelop adults as well. When the kids get tired of trying to hug a trunk that can accommodate eight adults linking hands, bedazzle them with a contorted red cedar known as "Canada's Gnarliest Tree." Keeping with the theme, it looks remarkably like Jabba the Hutt. Avatar Grove is located about ten kilometres outside of Port Renfrew in Pacheedaht territory, with half the road paved, and the rest a gravel logging road with some gnarly parts of its own (you'll want to take it easy with the speed). The trail through this remarkable old-growth

BIG, TALL, AND OLD

Canada's Largest Tree: The Cheewhat Giant is a western red cedar in Pacific Rim National Park Reserve. It soars 55.5 metres high, with a 5.84-metre diameter, and was first identified in 1988.

Canada's Oldest Tree: A larch tree in Manning Provincial Park, B.C., has been dated at over 1,900 years old. In 1980, a yellow cedar tree on B.C.'s Sunshine Coast was cut down, and dated at 1,835 years old. Its tourism value would have been worth so much more than lumber.

Canada's Tallest Tree: The Red Creek Fir is a contender — a towering Douglas fir located along the San Juan River near Port Renfrew, B.C., laser measured at 73.80 metres tall. The current title belongs to the Sitka spruce, 96 metres high and roughly six hundred years old, in the Carmanah Valley on Vancouver Island.

forest is often undergoing maintenance, so check online to see if it's open before you make the journey.

As more visitors arrive in search of forest giants, perhaps conditions — and signage — will improve. According to the Ancient Forest Alliance, a B.C. organization working to protect these natural wonders and support sustainable second-growth forestry practices, less than 25 percent of the old-growth forests capable of growing big trees on Vancouver Island still exist. Recent studies have shown that conserving old-growth trees has greater economic benefits in the long term than cutting them down. Avatar Grove, for example, has become an international tourist attraction, bolstering the local economy. With foreign markets insatiable for valuable old-growth timber, the logging industry and conservationists are bound to clash, sometimes violently. Just a few miles from Avatar Grove, the Fairy Creek Blockades of 2021 saw the arrest of over one thousand protesters, making it the largest act of civil disobedience in Canadian history. Fortunately, temperatures have cooled and voices have been heard. New measures have been taken to protect what little old growth remains, as the provincial and federal government work with First Nations across the province to pause logging on millions of hectares of remaining virgin forest.

Folks are passionate about these old giants, and when you see them, you'll understand why. Prepare to feel a distinct emotional and childlike awe in their presence. These spectacular survivors have seen much, and hopefully will continue to stand tall and see so much more. Go ahead and hug one.

STOP AND SMELL THE ROSES

A botanical wonderland

⚲ Butchart Gardens, Victoria
🔗 canadianbucketlist.com/butchartgardens

RECEIVING AROUND ONE MILLION VISITORS EACH YEAR, Vancouver Island's iconic Butchart Gardens is a National Historic Site, and a stunning depiction of flora as art. Set on fifty-five acres of privately owned land near Victoria, the gardens date back to 1904.

TOP 10 PLACES TO SEE FLOWERS IN WESTERN CANADA

Have a fancy for the floral? Water your passion with these options in Western Canada:

1. Butchart Gardens, Victoria, B.C.
2. Vancouver Cherry Blossom Festival, Vancouver, B.C.
3. Chilliwack Tulip Festival, Chilliwack, B.C.
4. Waterton Wildflower Festival, Waterton Lakes National Park, Alberta
5. Manning Provincial Park wildflowers, Manning Provincial Park, B.C.
6. Bradner Flower Show, Bradner, B.C.
7. Queen Elizabeth Park, Vancouver, B.C.
8. Prairie Gardens, Edmonton, Alberta
9. Nikka Yuko Japanese Garden, Lethbridge, Alberta
10. Dr. Sun Yat-Sen Classical Chinese Garden, Vancouver, B.C.

Having exhausted a limestone quarry for the family's successful business, matriarch Jennie Butchart was determined to restore the natural beauty of the area. Anyone who steps into her ivy-coated Sunken Garden can see just how seriously she took the task. Today, more than fifty gardeners maintain the immaculate Butchart Gardens, well-deserving of their world-renowned reputation. Open year-round, flowers and bulbs change with the seasons, blossoming by the thousands in spring, glowing in summer, radiating red and gold in the fall.

The gardens are also impressively committed to sustainability, with water conservation, soil renewal, and on-site recycling programs designed to protect, maintain, and nurture the gardens for future generations. Management have invested heavily in LED greenhouses, electric boat tours, diversified water sources, integrated pest management, and electric tools for its staff. All plant and food waste are composted and reused, drip irrigation is used extensively, only natural cleaning products are used, and staff are rewarded for carpooling to work.

On-site restaurants and tea gardens (serving organic, locally sourced products) keep visitors satiated, while a classic carousel brings out the kid in everyone (I think I enjoyed it more than my young kids). Most visitors spend about ninety minutes exploring the various gardens, but if you're not in a rush, take a blanket with you and stop to relax in the sunshine, surrounded by dancing bees and a riot of floral colour. Don't miss the Japanese Garden, the Italian Garden, the Rose Garden, live summer music performances, and fireworks on Saturday evenings in July and August.

UNCOVER THE WORLD OF WHISTLER

On and off the slopes

◎ Whistler

⌘ canadianbucketlist.com/whistler

WHEN IT COMES TO NORTH AMERICA'S LARGEST AND MOST highly rated ski resort, one word comes to mind: *epic*. Epic terrain. Epic snow. Epic dining. Epic partying. Between Whistler and the adjacent mountain, Blackcomb, you've got 8,100 acres of skiable terrain linked by the world's longest and highest lift system, the 4.4-kilometre-long Peak

2 Peak. That's over 50 percent more terrain than any other ski resort on the continent, and the reason you'll find visitors from around the world in the lineups. To snag the first line of the day, I pick up a First Tracks pass, which offers a breakfast buffet and early loading privileges at the top of the mountain. I've still got egg in my mouth when I hear "The runs are open!" This initiates a school bell–like atmosphere as everyone grabs their gear and races off to Emerald Express.

I'm not one for throwing myself into the challenging double diamond bowls, although there's plenty of that to go around. Rather, I choose my favourite blue runs: Harmony Ridge, Peak to Creek, the Saddle, and Spanky's Ladder. Riding the impressive Peak 2 Peak gondola can be unnerving, especially in the glass-bottom carriage. The reward — heaps of snow on Blackcomb with evocatively named lifts like Jersey Cream and, yes, Seventh Heaven — is worth it.

Beyond the slopes, Whistler is its own universe. Staggering growth has made it one of the planet's most popular mountain towns, lined by high-end fashion stores, ski shops, and outstanding restaurants. These days, the summer is busier than winter, as the town switches gears to become a mountain-biking mecca. You can visit the Audain Art Museum, a world-class gallery packed with Indigenous art, and the Squamish Lil'wat Cultural Centre for a fascinating glimpse into the region's cultural heritage. Each evening, Vallea Lumina transforms the dark forests on Cougar Mountain into a dazzling multimedia light show. Whistler also hosts an annual film festival, a writers festival, the World Ski and Snowboard Festival, a Pride and ski festival, Crankworx, and the Whistler Cornucopia food festival. Clubs and bars heave in peak winter and summer seasons, the most iconic being Garfinkel's, Dubh Linn Gate, Merlin's, Buffalo Bills, Moe Joe's, and Tommy Africa's. To skip the lineups, grab a ticket on an organized bar hop or pub crawl. If you want to retire early to catch first tracks, that's perfectly understandable too.

UNIQUE THRILLS IN WHISTLER

Bobsleigh or Skeleton: Calling all thrill-seekers — head to the Whistler Sliding Centre to hop in a bobsleigh as a passenger, bulleting through ten twists at speeds of up to 125 km/hr down the Olympic track. No experience is required to hop in, hold tight, and embrace the G-force. Not thrilling enough? Do it yourself, head-first, with the Public Skeleton. Launching farther down the track, you'll fly through six corners, clocking 100 km/hr and a whole lot more decibels as you scream all the way. It's over so fast they let you do it twice. Canada's only public skeleton experience is open December to April. I still can't believe I actually did it, and neither will you.

Zip-line Between the Mountains: An eight-minute drive from Whistler Village is Superfly, Canada's longest zip line. Fly backcountry-style between the soaring peaks of Cougar and Rainbow Mountains, and with tandem lines you can share the experience too. Using a comfortable harness more familiar to hang-gliders, hold on to a bar or go hands-free as you clock in at speeds of more than 100 km/hr. When you break free of the forest canopy, the scenery is simply astounding. Is it a bird? A plane? No, it's just you.

Just under half the accommodation options in Whistler are condos and house rentals, while hotels range from the high-end (Four Seasons, Fairmont, Westin, Nita Lake Lodge) to the centrally located Pangea Pod Hotel, creatively designed and packed with innovations for those on a budget. Throw a snowball in any direction and it will lead you to a great restaurant: iconic high-end establishments like Araxi, Bearfoot Bistro, and Il Caminetto; popular eateries like Sushi Village, Bar Oso, Alta Bistro, Hunter Gather, and Wild Blue; and après at Dusty's Bar & BBQ, High Mountain Brewing Co., Crystal Lounge, Garibaldi Lift Co. Bar and Grill, and the Longhorn Saloon.

There's a lot going on in Whistler, and the entire experience is significantly different from other ski resorts in Western Canada. Some people love it, others find it too big and busy. Some return year after year, or simply pack up and move here for good. Either way, no Western Canada bucket list would be complete without it.

STROLL THE SEAWALL

◎ Stanley Park, Vancouver

🔗 canadianbucketlist.com/stanleypark

"CAN YOU IMAGINE, SOME PEOPLE ACTUALLY LIVE HERE!"
I overheard that comment from one of the ten million people who visit Vancouver's Stanley Park every year, during my first stroll along its 8.8-kilometre paved seawall. When the sun is beaming, the park, and the city that it serves, just has that effect on people.

FLYOVER CANADA

🔗 *canadianbucketlist.com/flyover*

Want to fly but afraid of heights? Vancouver's FlyOver Canada is a fear-friendly simulation ride that puts you at the centre of a huge screen dome. You're safely strapped into your chair, the floor drops away, and soon you're whooshing through coastal rainforests and the Rockies, over cowboys in the Prairies, and into Niagara Falls. Engaging the rest of your senses, this "4D" eight-minute ride allows you to smell the scents and feel the mist and the wind. This bird's-eye view is delightfully overwhelming, great value, and fun for all ages. Another spectacular flight, entitled *Windborne: Call of the Canadian Rockies*, focuses on the iconic mountains along with some of the Indigenous legends associated with them.

Stanley Park is the first place I take visitors to Vancouver, because it's the first and most powerful impression I can give them. One second, we're surrounded by apartment buildings, and the next we're in a tranquil forest, with stellar views of the North Shore Mountains, or the sun reflecting off the glass of buildings downtown.

SEA VANCOUVER

🔗 *canadianbucketlist.com/seavancouver*

Vancouver joins Cape Town, Sydney, and Rio de Janeiro among the world's most beautiful cities. If you don't want to walk or cycle around Stanley Park, you can take a hop-on, hop-off bus, harbour cruise, floatplane flight, or visit the Vancouver Lookout tower. If you don't mind being out in the elements, I also recommend Sea Vancouver's Zodiac tour. Well-priced, with the fun bonus of bouncing over waves, the ninety-minute ride covers Coal Harbour, English Bay, False Creek, and Stanley Park. Weatherproof cruiser suits are provided, but wear layers for the wind.

If you look at the view of downtown and Stanley Park from across the Burrard Inlet on Spanish Banks, Stanley Park looks almost exactly the same size as downtown, a perfect balance between nature and city. With a half-million trees, two hundred kilometres of trails, and attractions such as a world-class aquarium, fantastic beaches, manicured gardens, a Pitch and Putt golf course, and concerts under the stars in Malkin Bowl, there's plenty to do in Stanley Park.

Some might argue — under their voices during hockey season — that this is Lord Stanley's greatest legacy. For our bucket list, simply walk or pedal around the seawall, taking in the views of mountains, city, ocean, birds, people. It's something to appreciate in all weather, but on a warm summer day, be prepared that it will likely make you want to live here too.

CROSS A SUSPENSION BRIDGE

Do look down

⛺ North Vancouver

🔗 canadianbucketlist.com/capilano

THE VIRAL POST READS: "13 BREATHTAKING PLACES Guaranteed to Make Your Stomach Drop."

It's a typical headline you often see in the clickbait frenzy of social media, although at least it isn't accompanied by "#5 made me laugh so hard I peed my pants." Naturally, I click on the link, where I find images

GOLDEN SKYBRIDGE

Not to be outdone, the town of Golden is home to the Golden Skybridge, an attraction that boasts two of the highest suspension bridges in the country, both with stellar views of the Columbia Valley, as well as the towering Rocky and Purcell Mountains. With a treetop canopy course, climbing wall, playground, canyon swing, zip line, and a kilometre-long mountain coaster, it's an action-packed, family-friendly roadside attraction on the Trans-Canada Highway between B.C. and Banff.

from truly scary spots in Norway, China, Zimbabwe, and Spain, most of which I've been to. But it's Number 10 on the list that stands out for me, for one very simple reason: it's one of the most popular and accessible tourist attractions in Vancouver.

Stretching 137 metres across North Vancouver's Capilano Canyon, the Capilano Suspension Bridge was originally built of hemp rope and cedar planks back in 1889. Since then, it has been completely

reconstructed as the centrepiece of a west coast outdoor ecotourist theme park, which includes a treetop platform path built amidst 1,300-year-old Douglas-fir trees, traditional totem poles, forest hikes, interpretation stations, and a series of cantilevered and suspended walkways constructed against a striking granite cliff. Seasonal events like Canyon Lights in winter or the mid-February Love Lights illuminate the entire park into a truly magical outdoor attraction.

Still, it's the suspension bridge that has drawn visitors for more than a century, swaying with every step, seventy metres above the Capilano River. Technically, there are longer suspension bridges out there that are not as high, and higher bridges that are not as long. But few bridges are run like this slick tourism operation, with its heavy tour-bus traffic in the summer and all-season appeal. Regardless of the viral attention, the Capilano Suspension Bridge will always wow her visitors, and claim a spot on *The Great Western Canada Bucket List*.

SLIDE DOWN THE MALAHAT SKYWALK

Spiralling in control

⚲ Malahat
🔗 canadianbucketlist.com/malahat

WHEN I TRAVELLED ACROSS AUSTRALIA RESEARCHING *THE Great Australian Bucket List*, I discovered that building and bridge climbs are incredibly popular Down Under. Canada, fortunately, is catching up. We have our fantastic suspension bridges, Toronto's CN Tower EdgeWalk, and the Glacier Skywalk in the Rockies. In 2021,

Vancouver Island welcomed the ten-storey-high Malahat Skywalk — a spiralling wooden tower that rises 250 metres above the Saanich Inlet. Entering through the gift shop, we walked along a six-hundred-metre raised wooden boardwalk, stopping to admire fantastic natural art, peeling arbutus trees, and creature art cleverly hidden in the bush below to engage the kids.

The scale and execution of the striking tower is instantly impressive. This is just not something you see every day. Inside, a twenty-metre-long spiralling metal slide immediately captured my daughter's attention, so she grabbed a slide rug to join the queue halfway up. While she waited, I continued the circular ascent with my son, listening to the whoops of sliders inside the tube. At the topmost viewing deck, interpretative boards taught us about the region's fauna, flora, and Indigenous history, enhanced by a sensational 360-degree view that just never quit. We found our own thrill crossing the Adventure Net with the world beneath us, and returned to the bottom just as my daughter popped out the slide with a big goofy smile. Of course, we *had* to head up again to show her the views and Adventure Net. I don't know who comes up with these wild ideas, but the appeal is undeniable, and if they're executed half as well as the Malahat Skywalk, I expect we'll always find space for them on our bucket list.

BRITISH COLUMBIA

RIDE A MOUNTAIN COASTER

On track for the summer season

◎ Revelstoke, North Vancouver, and around B.C.
∂ canadianbucketlist.com/coaster

THE IDEA OF A SKI RESORT TRANSFORMING ITSELF INTO A
four-season destination goes back decades, but the idea has exploded
with the popularity of mountain biking, hiking, golfing, and other
outdoor pursuits. Whistler has become busier in the summer than the
winter, and other resorts in Western Canada have taken note, looking

to extend their high seasons, increase their revenue, and expand their customer base. One of the more thrilling innovations to come out of all this is the mountain coaster, also known as an alpine coaster. Invented by a Swiss company in the 1990s, the idea is simple: Take a ski chair to the top of a mountain, strap into a small sled that is fixed onto a roller coaster–like metal track, and away you go! As the track swoops you through forest, tunnels, twists and turns, a simple brake lever lets you go as fast or slow as your nerves allow. It's completely safe — you won't disconnect from the track — but if you're pushing the forty-kilometres-per-hour speed limit you'll definitely feel the jolty turns on your hips. Young kids can sit between your legs, and you can expect big hollers and smiles all the way down. Rides are usually sold in packs because one descent won't be enough. Check out Revelstoke's Pipe Mountain Coaster, Cypress Mountain's Eagle Coaster, Golden's Railrider Mountain Coaster, and Canyon Ski Resort's 1,345-metre-long Canyon Coaster in Alberta.

CYCLE THE KVR

It's all downhill from here

⊚ Kelowna
⊘ canadianbucketlist.com/okanagan

HAVE YOU EVER DRIVEN PAST A CYCLIST STRUGGLING UP A HILL with loaded saddlebags? Pedalling through gorgeous countryside sounds fun, if not the thought of being *that* sweating cyclist. Perhaps, like me, you'd prefer a cycling adventure without the punishing physicality. Is it possible to have our cake with the bike forks to eat it too? It is.

Opened in 1915, the Kettle Valley Railway was the primary means of transportation through the rugged mountains, valleys, and lakes of southern B.C. Building five hundred kilometres of track across this terrain was a feat of extraordinary engineering and no easy task: it involved thousands of immigrant labourers slogging in back-breaking, often deadly conditions. Somehow, they blasted tunnels, traversed perilous cliffs, and engineered some of the most striking wooden trestles in North America. By 1964, highways had eliminated the passenger service, and in 1989, the Kettle Valley Railway was discontinued altogether. With the tracks removed, the KVR was reinvented as a rail trail, shepherding cyclists and hikers through the Okanagan region with a maximum 2.2 percent grade. Translation: no hills, easy riding, and a bucket-list cycling adventure for everyone. Especially when a company provides bikes, accommodation, an excellent self-guided trail app, and shuttles your bags ahead.

Ottawa-based Great Canadian Trails (GCT) does the logistical heavy lifting, so expect less time sweating the details, and more time enjoying the views. Although the terrain is mostly flat, I choose an e-bike because I'm as fit as a bag of Flamin' Hot Cheetos. The shuttle collects me in West Kelowna, where my itinerary begins at a lovely B&B with a sweeping vista of Okanagan Lake. My e-bike has a comfortably wide seat, an easy-to-operate pedal-assist system, and a saddlebag for water, sunblock, and packed lunches. From here, it's about an hour's drive to the trailhead near Idabel Lake, and onto the KVR we go.

It's downhill all the way to the KVR's rockstar highlight: the Myra Canyon Trestles. Entering this B.C. provincial park and National Historic Site, the gravel trail takes a twelve-kilometre one-way stretch across eighteen wooden trestles and through two rock tunnels. The views of the valley and mountains are extraordinary, as is the fact that volunteers rebuilt several trestles after a devastating wildfire in 2003.

Some are longer and higher than others, but all provide a thrilling crossing. Day visitors to the park can rent bikes at the trailhead, but I continue along the KVR toward my lakeside accommodation.

While the gradient is kind, the gravel trail does get a little choppy in spots. Still, there's no rush as I make my way through lush forest bursting with the colours of fireweed, balsamroot, wild rose, and lupine. Using my phone's GPS (no cellphone coverage is required), the trail app lets me track my progress, and it's all but impossible to get lost. My bag is waiting for me inside a comfortable glamping tent when I get to Chute Lake Lodge, along with a cold craft beer, a refreshing swim in the tea-coloured lake, and a pub-style dinner. Since I don't ride much, my butt feels a little tender, but any exercise makes you feel good at the end of the day. I sleep like a resting boulder.

Day 2 is a forty-kilometre ride along the KVR to Penticton, and I can't help but wonder how today could possibly top Day 1. Substitute mountains for dense pine forest and sparkling lakes, that's how. The

WINE IN B.C.

British Columbia produces over sixty types of varietals, the most popular reds being Merlot, Pinot Noir, and Cabernet Sauvignon, and the most popular whites Pinot Gris, Chardonnay, and Gewürztraminer. The province has five major wine regions: the Okanagan Valley, the Similkameen Valley, the Fraser Valley, Vancouver Island, and the Gulf Islands.

gentle downhill slope makes the riding particularly easy, and at times, almost meditative. I roll into the vineyards and bursting orchards of the Naramata Bench around noon, stopping at the excellent Abandoned Rail Brewing Co. for lunch and a refreshing dry-hopped lager. Tonight's B&B is right off the trail, and nearby vineyards like Red Rooster, Ruby Blues, D'Angelo, and Little Engine make for a fine afternoon wine-tasting session. I hop back on the KVR to ride downhill into Penticton for dinner, confident the e-bike will take care of the hill back to the B&B.

In the morning, a shuttle drops me at the trailhead for the final day's ride. The KVR cuts through wild sage bush from Summerland to Penticton, along the Penticton channel, and onto a trail that circumnavigates Skaha Lake. I stop for lunch at the Historic Okanagan Falls Hotel (now the OK Falls Hotel), and ride back along a paved, twisty road to rejoin the KVR to my B&B on the Naramata Bench.

Over three days, GCT had curated the very best 150 kilometres of the KVR. The Okanagan, one of Canada's largest fruit and wine-producing regions, is a magnificent part of the world. Taking it in by bicycle — without sweat or slog — is a welcome bucket-list adventure for cycling, wine, outdoor, and history buffs.

JET BOAT ON THE SKEENA

Deep views from shallow water

📍 Terrace

🔗 canadianbucketlist.com/skeena

BRITISH COLUMBIA IS AN ONION, AND WITH EACH JOURNEY into its bucket list, I'm peeling back a layer. This might explain why my eyes are watering as the jet boat slowly hums up the turquoise Exchamsiks River. Maybe it's just the wind.

"If the Icefields Parkway [see page 124] is the most beautiful road in the country, then surely this must be the country's most beautiful river," I tell

72

Rob Bryce of Northern BC Jet Boat Tours. Not any old boat can explore these shallow waters. I glance at the depth gauge and somehow we're coasting above just half a metre of water. Flowing into the mighty Skeena, B.C.'s second longest river, the Exchamsiks has seen many a vessel run aground on its shallow sandy bottom, although you can't blame boaters for giving it a go. The overwhelming views kick in as soon as you turn off the wide Skeena, which isn't lacking in the scenic department either.

Invented in New Zealand, jet boats are propelled by water, which means they don't have an outboard engine and propeller below. It also makes them exceptionally powerful — the fastest jet boats have the acceleration power of an F-16 fighter jet. In the shallow, narrow channel, Rob is understandably gentle on the throttle of his 430-horsepower Thunder Cat.

"You should see what this place looks like in late spring," explains Rob. "We're surrounded by waterfalls in every direction."

As with all northern rivers, the landscape here can dramatically change with the season. We navigate up the stream, each bend delivering a postcard view, until a large fallen tree blocks the way, causing a sandbank that even a jet boat can't cross. It's late August, and after an unseasonably dry summer, the Exchamsiks is running lower than usual. Rob also has inflatable jet boats, which he employs in just such a situation to continue the adventure, but today we're a large group with less time on our hands. Rob parks the boat on a sandbar and quickly gets to work gathering wood for a lunchtime picnic.

I see countless eagles overhead and several bears on the shore, while migrating coho salmon leap out the water in the shadow of dramatic rock shelves. Rob is an enthusiastic host with a deep appreciation for the region, and plenty of hard-won experience piloting jet boats on a particularly challenging river that demands a veteran's touch. There are places in Canada that bring a tear to the eye, no onions needed. On a clear, blue-sky late-summer day, northern British Columbia is full of them.

DINE ACROSS THE DIVIDE

Unique dishes for a unique region

📍 Vancouver

🔗 canadianbucketlist.com/bannock

VANCOUVER IS A WORLD-CLASS CITY INCREASINGLY recognized for its world-class cuisine. In late 2022, eight restaurants received the city's first distinguished Michelin stars. These were the Quebecois-inspired St. Lawrence, the Chinese iDen & QuanJuDe Beijing Duck House, the Japanese Masayoshi, and contemporary restaurants Published on Main, AnnaLena, Barbara, and Burdock and Co. As one might expect, all use premium, locally sourced ingredients, but other than showcasing B.C.'s outstanding seafood, would their menus be out of place in Quebec, China, Japan, or inside other fine-dining restaurants worldwide? No. If you're looking for food of the land, food of the people, and food for thought, the restaurant to put on your bucket list is Salmon n' Bannock. Visit the only Indigenous restaurant in Vancouver, and stop and smell the sage bush.

Located on West Broadway and tastefully decorated with Indigenous artwork, there's a big heart at the centre of this small restaurant, and a story with every dish. It starts with a one-year-old girl swept up in the Sixties Scoop — a horrendous era when government authorities forcibly removed Indigenous kids from their homes. Inez Cook was taken from her Nuxalk community in Bella Coola and placed in foster care. Raised by loving white parents, she grew up with little connection to her Indigenous roots. As a flight attendant, she lived and travelled around the world, falling in love with cuisine, while nurturing a growing curiosity about her past. Salmon n' Bannock is the result.

When Inez launched the restaurant in 2010, she was welcomed back by the Nuxalk, and has used great food to bring people together ever since. It's a bold and confident act of what she calls *reconcilli-action*. Her friendly staff and kitchen crew serve up a unique menu of dishes native to the region, creatively adapted for discerning and adventurous urban palettes.

"Indigenous people used what was locally available," she tells me over an alluring plate of appetizers. "Farm-to-table, the 100-mile diet — we were the OG trendsetters!"

With glowing reviews and profiles in global media including the *New York Times*, CNN, and BBC, Salmon n' Bannock is a fantastic story that literally breaks bread across the cultural divide. But you can't eat a story, so what's on the plate?

Hot smoked candied salmon with maple, cracked pepper, and delicate sweetgrass-infused cherries. Light elk salami and rich duck terrine. Citrusy salmon ceviche, double smoked cheese, homemade pickles, and the #addictive wild BBQ salmon mousse. Baked *bannock* — which Inez corrects me rhymes with *panic* — makes a wonderful cracker, smothered with her updated version of traditional pemmican: smoked bison with sage-infused blueberries and cream cheese. I wash it down with a refreshing Bella Coola soda, infused with hibiscus, rosehips, orange, and apple. No chance I'll get to the bison pot roast, game sausage, Anishinaabe risotto, smoked sablefish, or urban sage-smoked salmon burger. One visit won't cut it.

It's healthy, sustainable, and delicious, so when will Indigenous cuisine share a food court with other international cuisines? This is not a theme, Inez reminds me. "It gets me from zero to a thousand in lividness when we're called a theme restaurant. Japanese or Italian food is not a theme. Indigenous is not a theme. We are living cultures."

There are only a handful of Indigenous restaurants across Western Canada, but they're winning both fans and awards. Scott Jonathan Iserhoff's Pei Pei Chei Ow café in Edmonton won Best Trailblazer in *enRoute*'s list of Canada's Best New Restaurants. You'll find the Kekuli Café in Merritt and West Kelowna, Bear & Bone Burger Co. in Golden, the Ktunaxa Grill at the Ainsworth Hot Springs, and several others. Those flying out of Vancouver can leave with a taste too: Salmon n' Bannock opened a second location in the international departures lounge of YVR. Business is strong, but there are still challenges.

"You might have bad Chinese food one day, but that won't stop you ever eating Chinese food again. People have to get familiar with our food. We only get one shot," she says.

Yes, Vancouver is blessed with dozens of fantastic restaurants (and we don't need Michelin to tell us). Yet crafting great food through an Indigenous lens, and doing it responsibly with the full support of the community, suggests we're heading toward a promising, and uniquely regional, culinary future. Enjoy the feast.

INDIGENOUS EXPERIENCES FOR THE B.C. BUCKET LIST

Klahoose Wilderness Resort: An off-the-grid intimate eco-resort located in Desolation Sound, Klahoose specializes in all-inclusive wilderness packages for spring bear tours, the salmon run, grizzly bear viewing, and year-round cultural and wildlife packages.

Haida House at Tllaal: Offers all-inclusive week-long adventure packages (with a fantastic dining room), creating an ideal base to explore the natural attractions, and historical and cultural sites found on Haida Gwaii's Graham and Moresby Islands.

Squamish Lil'wat Cultural Centre in Whistler: Showcases the fascinating art, history, and traditions of the Squamish and Lil'wat Nations, and features regular exhibits, guided tours, and hands-on workshops.

Tofino: Stay at the Tin Wis Resort and take the Tofino Art Gallery Walk, which includes the House of Himwitsa First Nations Art Gallery and Roy Henry Vickers Gallery. Whale-watch and visit sacred pools with the Indigenous-owned Clayoquot Wild.

Skwachàys Lodge: The first Indigenous boutique art hotel in Vancouver, the lodge showcases Indigenous art and culture. The hotel and gallery have an Indigenous artist in residence, with workshops including beading, drum making, rattle making, and carving.

Ainsworth Hot Springs Resort: Soak in the *nupika wu'u*, or hot mineral waters, first enjoyed by the Ktunaxa peoples after hunting, fishing, or gathering. Owned by the Lower Kootenay Band of Creston, the resort includes complimentary access to the pools and cave.

The Museum of Anthropology at UBC: Showcases the art and culture of Indigenous communities from across B.C. and around the world, with over fifty thousand ethnographic objects, including carvings, masks, and textiles.

The Nk'mip Desert Cultural Centre: A nine-thousand-square-foot interpretive centre with indoor and outdoor exhibits, a 1.5-kilometre walking trail, and a reconstructed traditional Okanagan village. Interpreter programs are designed to appeal to all ages.

RIDE HARD AND LIVE FREE

B.C. and the art of motorcycle maintenance

⊙ Bella Coola to Vancouver
⊘ canadianbucketlist.com/harley

IF YOU SEE A MOTORCYCLE PASS ANOTHER ON THE HIGHWAY,
look closely. You'll notice that riders of all stripes greet each other with
a subtle hand gesture. On B.C.'s spectacular highways, it's more than
just an acknowledgement of the exhilaration of motorcycle riding: it's
a celebration of riders' good fortune to be riding *these* roads, in this

magical part of Canada. The bike salute binds riders into a Fellowship of Road Trips. Blink and you'll miss it.

Perhaps, like me, you don't own a motorcycle, and never have. Perhaps, like me, you're drawn to the experience of riding a Harley on some of the country's most scenic roads. Perhaps you're *also* nervous about high speeds or dumb risks, or not willing to drop thousands of dollars on a bike you'll rarely use. Tucked off Vancouver's Marine Drive is the only Canadian outlet of the Harley-Davidson–owned EagleRider Rentals & Tours. They offer diverse models, unlimited mileage, one-way itineraries, a generous membership program, and full insurance with roadside support.

Ninety percent of their business is international riders, drawn to the epic highways of B.C. and the enduring allure of Harley-Davidson. Clients can pick from dozens of new models, including electric bikes, three-wheelers, and old-school roadsters. I opted for the classic yet powerful 1,746-cc Road King, forgoing bells and whistles so I could focus on the road. The membership program secured my bike for about a hundred dollars a day, gas and insurance included. Now I needed a road trip.

Bikers find each other because it's fun, and safer, to travel in groups. Riding in staggered formation, groups own the road and rarely get overtaken. I was fortunate to join (let's avoid the word "crash") an annual road trip of a group ranging in age from twenty-four to sixty. They'd spent months planning a trip north from Victoria, taking the ten-hour ferry to Bella Coola and returning south via Vancouver over five days. We met up along Vancouver Island's Highway 19, allowing me to get familiar with the bike, lifestyle, and landscape. In cars, we're encapsulated in a closed box as the world passes by. On the motorbike, I was fully immersed in the moment. We roll into Dave's Bakery in Campbell River, devour the best Reuben sandwich on the island, and discuss the trip ahead. Bikers are like anglers, eager to share war stories,

tips, and the odd tall tale. All agree my Harley is the most powerful bike in the group, worthy of admiration, and a fair amount of ribbing too. The Harley subculture deservedly tends to inspire both envy and ridicule. We haul up the coast, traffic dissipating as the meandering asphalt cuts through endless boreal forest. We pull off to look at roadside attractions and viewpoints. Sometimes we open up our throttles, sometimes we ride well below the speed limit in formation. Although my motorbike experience is limited at best, I feel safe in the leather saddle, and grateful for the Road King's forgiving clutch. We arrive in Port Hardy to spend the night in the excellent Kwa'lilas Hotel, looking forward to the early morning ferry.

BC Ferries' Northern Sea Wolf is a seventy-six-metre-long vessel offering year-round service between Port Hardy and Bella Coola and taking just thirty-five cars and 150 passengers and crew. We reserved months in advance — the spacious ferry fills up in the summer months with RVs and campers. We board the 7:30 a.m. boat, strapping our

THE BEST RIDES IN WESTERN CANADA

The Sea to Sky Highway (Highway 99, B.C.): Vancouver to Whistler with throttle-stopping views of the Pacific, mountains, and waterfalls.

Pacific Rim Highway (Highway 4, B.C.): Tree tunnels, road twists, beaches, mountains, and ocean air from Port Alberni to Tofino.

Kananaskis Trail (Highway 40, Alberta): Tracking the eastern slopes of the Rockies, with amazing views of mountains, valleys, and rivers.

Cowboy Trail (Highway 22, Alberta): A gorgeous stretch along the foothills of the Rockies, taking in the prairies, mountains, and sweeping ranches.

Lillooet to Cache Creek (Highway 99, B.C.): Across the arid canyons, through mountain passes and fertile valleys, and snaking along the mighty Fraser River.

David Thompson Highway (Highway 11, Alberta): Mountain magic with stunning views of lakes, mountains, and waterfalls.

Castlegar-Nelson-Creston Highway (Highway 3A, B.C.): Scenic forests, mountains, and lakes on the western shore of Kootenay Lake.

Banff to Radium Hot Springs (Highway 93, Alberta): Through Banff and Kootenay National Parks, in the long shadows of mountains and glaciers.

bikes down to counter strong waves that fortunately do not materialize. On the upper deck, we join tourists taking in the extraordinary coastline, framed by King Island and soaring cliffs on the mainland. The captain makes regular announcements about whale sightings, and a humpback breaches as if on cue. It's a long, comfortable journey; we play cards, chat with travellers, gaze at the channel, and look forward to the challenge ahead.

We strike out early the next day from Bella Coola, anticipating issues along Highway 20's infamous Hill full of switchbacks, steep inclines, single-lane passes, and hard-packed gravel. Unseasonal wet weather has created long stretches of choppy mud. Our group's hybrid off-road bikers lick their lips, but I decide to call a friend in Williams Lake, who borrows a trailer to help my rental Harley over the swampy hill. No need to be a hero. Although the Harley brand promises renegade freedom, the truth is that most Harley riders are not outlaws Wanted Dead or Alive. They're wanted back in the office on Monday morning.

I rejoin my mud-baked group at the other side of the Hill. We fuel up in Nimpo Lake and speed out into a long, wild biking day with everything: sun, rain, mud, curves, flats, horses, cows, and the shadows of moose. Lush farmland, burned forests, snow-capped peaks, marmots,

and mosquitoes the size of marmots. South from Williams Lake, the topography is more dramatic. Sagebrush bristles in the breeze as we snake through narrow mountain canyons carved by the mighty Fraser River. Dozens of bikers gather in Lillooet for the night, heading north or south. We admire machines, compare road conditions and itineraries. On the final stretch, we wind our way to Pemberton and onward to Vancouver, riding the world-renowned Sea to Sky Highway. Eighteen hundred kilometres and five incredible days later, I return my Road King to EagleRider, greeting staff with a big smile. Whether you used to ride, want a different ride, or harbour a dream to conquer the open road, renting a motorbike in Vancouver is an affordable, easy, and magical opportunity. When you see me on the road next year, don't forget to wave.

UNUSUAL NATURAL ATTRACTIONS

Spot the Spotted Lake

📍 Kamloops

CANADA HAS OVER THREE MILLION LAKES, AND TEN KILO-metres west of Osoyoos, you'll find the strangest one of all. Hundreds of circular spots stretch across the aptly named Spotted Lake, containing highly concentrated minerals that often paint the pools in different colours. They're more visible in the summer, when the lake's water evaporates, leaving behind yellow, blue, and green pools. Dense in magnesium, sodium sulphate, calcium, and other minerals, the pools were mined to make ammunition during the First World War. The Syilx People of the Okanagan Nation call it Lake Kliluk, and they believe each pool has a different healing property. Although the lake is on private property, it can be easily seen from a viewpoint off Highway 3.

Get Spooked at the Skook

📍 Sunshine Coast

In local Chinook Jargon, "skookum" means "strong," and "chuck" means "water." When the tide changes daily in the narrow straight connecting the Sunshine Coast's Sechelt and Jervis Inlets, a powerful surge of seawater begins to flow in the opposite direction. The water rushes at up to 33 km/hr across a two-metre-high divide, creating epic rapids, whirlpools, and a unique geographic phenomenon. The powerful whirlpools safely suck in extreme kayakers, curious boaters, and even divers. It's definitely something to see, and not too difficult to do so. Skookumchuck Narrows Provincial Park, located in Egmont, has an easy four-kilometre trail leading to two viewing areas.

FLOAT A RIVER CHANNEL

Gently down the stream

⚲ Penticton

⊘ canadianbucketlist.com/tube

MANY YEARS AGO, I SPENT AN AFTERNOON FLOATING on a rubber tube down the Mekong River in Laos, toasting fellow floaters with cold beer, waving to locals on the riverbank, and celebrating my good fortune. I thought I'd have to return to Vang Vieng for that simple pleasure until I saw the river channel linking

MANY RIVERS TO FLOAT

Penticton is not the only place to blow up a tube and soak in the sunlight. Go with the flow in these rivers around the province:

The Cowichan River (Vancouver Island): The Tube Shack rents floaties for a two-and-a-half-hour ride along crystal-clear waters.

The Similkameen River (Princeton): Take four to five hours to float between Bromley Rock and Red Bridge, or use a long hot day to continue to Pine Park in Keremeos.

The Puntledge River (Courtenay): A local summer tradition in the Comox Valley, floats range from quick and fun runs in Puntledge Park, to a longer float concluding in Lewis Park.

The Alouette River (Maple Ridge): Bring your own floaties for an eleven-kilometre-long stretch that floats you to the Davidson's Pool and Hot Rocks swimming holes.

The Shuswap River (Enderby): With both a short and more rugged longer option, float between Mabel and Mara Lakes, through forests, canyons, and farmland.

Okanagan Lake and Skaha Lake in Penticton.

Rubber tubes were floating down the canal like twirling Froot Loops in a bowl of cherry cola. Every summer, the seven-kilometre channel fills with locals and visitors. Gliding on your back in the sun, perhaps with a clandestine bottle of wine chilling in a cooler at your side, it can take three to four hours to float the entire length. A handy shuttle service will return you to the entrance parking.

Any inner tube, air mattress, raft, or floating device will suffice, available at stores around town or for rent from Coyote Cruises, including a quad floater for those seeking maximum comfort. The water is shallow and safe, with a halfway point to exit in case the sun is a bit much or the weather turns. Penticton's river channel is not a water park, but the fortunate by-product of a dredge built to control flooding in the 1950s. It's relaxing as hell, and can be as social or meditative as you wish. If you're lumped with a loud group of spotty teenagers, pull to the side in the two-metre-deep water and give them some distance. It may not be as exotic as the Mekong River, but the accommodation and dining choices in Penticton are much better, trust me.

SPELUNK ON THE ISLAND

Getting down and dirty

📍 Horne Lake, Nanaimo
🔗 canadianbucketlist.com/hornelake

FOR MILLENNIA, EARLY HUMANS FOUND SANCTUARY IN DARK, quiet, and cool caves, escaping hostile elements and adapting to life underground. Spelunking reconnects us with this primeval ecosystem, and there are many ways and places to do it. I've had caving adventures in Belize, Budapest, New Zealand, the Cook Islands, Australia, and

BRITISH COLUMBIA

South Africa, ranging from challenging underwater caves to massive show caves welcoming large crowds on boardwalks. Ideally, you're looking for something the whole family can experience, but with enough tight squeezes to make it feel like a real adventure.

Millions of years ago, Vancouver Island was located on the ocean floor. About 4 percent of the island is limestone karst — an ideal geology for water to erode rock and create a subterranean network. The island has over one thousand recorded caves, more than all the caves discovered in Canada's other provinces *combined*. Some caves have over ten kilometres of mapped passages, which is why this "Island of Caves" is popular with spelunkers from around the world.

The best introduction to this underground ecosystem are the Horne Lake Caves, located between Nanaimo and Courtenay. The on-site tour operator offers various packages ranging in difficulty, although all are rugged and require hard hats, headlamps, overalls, scrambling, ducking, sliding, and squeezing. Since age limits apply and I have my young kids in tow, I leave the Max Depth Adventure (rappelling down a seven-storey underwater waterfall!) for another day, but the two-hour family-friendly Riverbend Cave Explorer tour is perfect. We descend a steep ladder into the dim world below, filled with peanut butter–coloured rock and crystal formations, stalactites, and soda straws. The hard hats come in handy more than once, and we get enough confined twisty action to keep everyone engaged. Older kids and more flexible adults will want to take on the longer and more intimidating Action Pack or Achilles Challenge, which involve belly crawls, cable ladder climbs, rappels, and gut-sucking squeezes. All will get to turn off their headlamps to experience pure, immaculate darkness of the world beneath our feet.

CLIMB THE GRIND

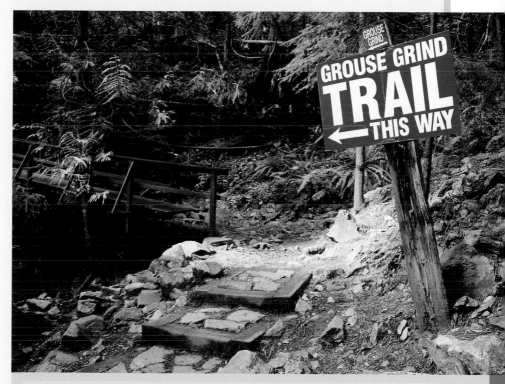

Mother Nature's StairMaster

📍 North Vancouver
🔗 canadianbucketlist.com/grind

VANCOUVERITES HAVE A SPECIAL PLACE IN THEIR HEARTS for physical pursuits. These are people obsessed with the outdoors, since it's among the best cities in the country, weather-wise, in which to enjoy it. Despite the "granola with my yoga" reputation, Vancouver also offers more demanding physical challenges. Take the

Grouse Grind, running 853 metres up the side of Grouse Mountain over exactly 2.9 kilometres.

At some point in your life, you've been physically exhausted — leg muscles burning, sweat stinging your eyes, mind full of blame. Well done, you've just reached the soul-crushing *quarter-way* sign on the Grouse Grind. The Grind is a walk in the park, and by "walk" I mean slog, and by "park" I mean mountain. In front of and behind you, you'll see others stuck in the same elevator from hell, but not to worry, everyone is too polite to panic. What's more, many will be dressed in form-fitting stretchy pants, because the Grouse Grind is not only a natural workout, it's an unlikely pickup joint for yuppies hell-bent on maximizing the tone of their glutes.

Among the one hundred thousand people who undertake the Grind every year, count on seeing at least one of the following during your visit:

- A young parent seriously regretting the genius idea of doing the Grind with a toddler on their back.
- Tourists who heard it's one of the city's most popular hikes, and have no idea what they are getting into. Typically wearing sandals.
- A hiker well into his or her seventies who seems to be having no trouble whatsoever.
- Pure despair when hikers reach the quarter-mark sign.
- Someone arriving at the sad realization that there's no view, and nowhere to go but up.

Regular Grinders time themselves, with the average being about ninety minutes, and the current record an astonishing twenty-three minutes and forty-eight seconds. In 2019, a fifty-seven-year-old engineer did the Grind nineteen times in nineteen hours as a

fundraiser challenge. My personal best up the 2,830 uneven dirt stairs is fifty-five minutes, but to be fair, I was drunk and in the mood for self-loathing. The reward for your calorie-decimating workout is typically beer and nachos at the Grouse Mountain bar. Having burnt off the calories, you'll replace them with interest. Fortunately, it's only ten dollars for the gondola ride down to the parking lot, where you'll find a mix of exhausted, sweaty hikers, and tourists trying not to touch them. If a Vancouverite asks to take you on the Grind, be prepared for a physical gauntlet. Or lie, with the reliable excuse, "I've done it, and once was enough!"

SUMMIT THE LIONS

Where legends are born

⚲ Lions Bay

🔗 canadianbucketlist.com/lions

THE LIONS ARE THE MOST DISTINCTIVE MOUNTAINS OVER-
looking Vancouver, named in the 1880s because they resemble two
sleeping lions, and because nobody back then deferred to more
significant Indigenous names. The East and West Lion peaks (reaching
1,605 metres and 1,645 metres respectively) inspired the BC Lions

football team, Lions Gate Bridge, Lions Gate Hospital, and movie studio Lions Gate Entertainment. They also inspire ambitious hikers to brave a knee-punishing ascent with a memorable day hike or overnight trek, complete with a challenging summit free-climb.

Before we get to the hike, it's important to recognize that these are not lions at all. According to the Squamish people, the peaks are markers of peace, formed by the Creator to honour a treaty between the Squamish and Haida peoples. Another legend involves twin sisters. While I'll call them Lions moving forward, it's important to recognize their Indigenous legacy.

There are two ways to hike the beasts. Park at Cypress Mountain ski resort and hike up and across the mountains, or park in Lions Bay and hike up … and up and up. The Cypress route adds a few kilometres and requires some parking and driving coordination. The Lions Bay route requires a lucky parking spot in the few public spots at the trailhead, or the addition of some asphalt road ascent to your journey. Signs at the trailhead to West Lion leave little doubt what's in store. Difficulty: Strenuous. *Only to be attempted by properly equipped and experienced hikers.* It's a fifteen-kilometre round trip, with a hefty 1,525-metre elevation gain. Signs suggest you budget an ambitious seven to eight hours. Up we go. And up. And up farther still. Poles and frequent water breaks are essential. Loose rocks and slippery roots lie in ambush. We cross a bridge over a fetching cascade, inviting a cool dip in the rock pools, but there's no time. It's an unseasonal warm, dry October, which means a lovely cool temperature and few bugs, but also shorter days. We were on the trail by 7:45 a.m. (The parking lot was already full.)

The West Lion is more accessible and a popular hike. Everyone I meet seems in better physical and mental shape to do it than me. After almost four hours, we crest at a viewpoint and finally see the mighty Lions up close. Solid rock (hornblende diorite for you geologists), the peaks are more imposing when you stand beneath them. As we press on, the rocks become bigger and more challenging, remnants of millennia of rockslides. Finally, we reach a large outcrop where most sane people stop to enjoy the incredible 360-degree-view of the Lions, Howe Sound, and, on a clear day, the city of Vancouver below. Most sane people will now say they've hiked the Lions, and call it a day. Others will continue on the twenty-nine-kilometre Howe Sound Crest Trail from Cypress Mountain to Porteau Cove, or tackle risky free-climb up to the West Lion summit. Cramping legs, blistered ankles, no fitness whatsoever … of course I'm going for the top.

Other than one handy rope to assist with an early five-metre drop, there are no ladders or ropes. I navigate up and over sheer rock, balancing on narrow ledges while desperately searching for rock holds, trying not to think about the thirty-to-fifty-metre plummet below. Some hikers have helmets and climbing shoes. I have a flask of rum. It's been a while since a physical challenge intersected so concisely with my mental fear, and several times I pause to breathe and recollect myself in that special place we all visit sometimes. It doesn't take very long to reach the summit, but after a challenging five-hour ascent, it's tough as hell. My thighs cramp up as I collapse in a heap by the West Lion's rock cairn, the only sign that I am, indeed, as high as one can go. It's almost enough to make me forget that I now have to get back down, and then descend a trail that knees have nightmares about.

A few Band-Aids, a swig of rum, sandwiches, painkillers, and we're headed down. Hell on your knees and tricky on the ankles, yet with fine company, fine weather, and the intangible joy of accomplishment, we slowly make our way down to Lions Bay. Sure, it would have helped to have prepared with more than just a few games of pickleball. As I lie in bed that night groaning, my wife asks me why on earth anybody would do this to themselves. "Every time I see those Lions," I reply, "I can think, 'I've ticked that off my bucket list!'"

RIDE THE SEA TO SKY GONDOLA

Howe's the view

🔖 Squamish

🔗 canadianbucketlist.com/seatosky

SQUAMISH'S SEA TO SKY GONDOLA OPENS UP ASTOUNDING views of Howe Sound, Sky Pilot Mountain, and the mighty Stawamus Chief itself. The 849-metre-long gondola ride takes you right to the top of an adjacent mountain, where you'll find a sixty-five-metre-high suspension bridge and scenic walking loops, as well as hiking and biking trails. Enjoy craft beer on the sunny patio with one of the best views in the province. An international climbing mecca and stopover on the way to Whistler, Squamish is a vibrant community offering wind sports, rafting, mountain biking, hiking, fishing, snowshoeing, and eagle-watching opportunities.

PAN FOR GOLD DUST

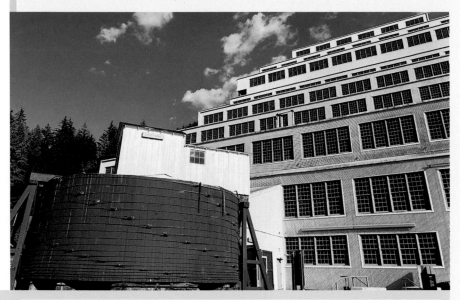

Rule Britannia

📍 Britannia Beach, south of Squamish
🔗 canadianbucketlist.com/britannia

ONE OF THE BETTER B.C. ROADSIDE ATTRACTIONS IS THE Britannia Mine Museum, a National Historic Site located along the Sea to Sky Highway. During its operation from 1904 to 1974, Britannia was one of the largest copper mines in the world, and the centre of a thriving community. The museum is a hands-on visit: explore the twenty-storey gravity-fed ore-processing plant (which houses a fantastic sound-light show), don overalls and a hard hat to head underground via train into a haulage tunnel, play traditional games, check out the massive giant haul truck, and pan for gold and gemstones.

FLY FISH WITH A HELICOPTER

Catch, release, repeat

⚲ Terrace
🔗 canadianbucketlist.com/helifish

PLACE THE WORD "HELI" BEFORE ANY OUTDOOR PURSUIT and it instantly becomes more fun.

Consider: heli-*skiing* (see pages 39–40), heli-*hiking*, or even heli-*biking*. I've heli-*swum* in alpine lakes you'd need days to hike to, taken a class of heli-*yoga*, and we can now add heli-*fishing* to the list.

Located outside of Terrace, the Northern Escape Mountain Lodge typically attracts heli-skiers to the Skeena and Coastal Mountain Ranges, with promises of deep powder, alpine bowls, massive glaciers, and endless virgin snow. With short, daily flights out of Vancouver, it's the province's most accessible heli-ski operation. In summer, the boutique lodge flips to offer wildlife viewing, mountain biking, jet-boat excursions (see pages 72–73), and ghost-town cultural tours (see page 103). But the biggest draw are the migrating steelhead trout and salmon that swell the region's waterways. With a bird's-eye view from the Agusta Koala helicopter, the reason for Skeena's world-renowned reputation as a bucket-list angling destination becomes immediately obvious.

Soaring above dense forest, I spot black bears lounging on riverbeds, with an astonishing abundance of food at their paw tips. Sky Richard, my experienced and aptly named heli-fishing guide, points out spawning beds and virgin fishing beaches. Some are simply inaccessible, while others would take hours to access by water. Sky directs the pilot to land at a particular spot on the Dala River, telling us all to keep an eye out for "G-bears." As the helicopter descends, I see shadows of fish darting among the rapids. The rapids aren't made by rocks, but by the sheer volume of salmon migrating upstream. There is indeed a G-bear up ahead, but it scatters into the dense bush as soon as we arrive. We're going to borrow the bear's spot for a couple hours, and his fish as well. Since it's strictly catch-and-release, Mr. G-Bear's meal will be here waiting when he returns.

I'm new to fly-fishing, but I still harbour visions from the Robert Redford film *A River Runs Through It*. Based on Norman Maclean's classic novella, it's a meditation on family, love, loss, and the draw of the rod.

"There was no clear line between religion and fly fishing," wrote Maclean, capturing the passion and mystique behind the pursuit. As I attempt to cast into the stream, I'm more concerned with the line lassoing Sky Richard's eyeball. He patiently shows me how to roll, Spey, and quick cast, and how to lower my rod and strip the flyline to mimic an attractive shrimp. Knee-deep in the water, I cast upstream, and let the current take my fly into the shadows. I don't have to wait long.

"I've got one!" "Got one!" "Got another!" "Got one!" "Here's another!" When you land a helicopter by a pristine mountain stream in a wilderness that nobody else can access, there's *a lot* of fish. You cast, you catch, and then release the fish to continue its spawning journey. Much thought goes into the type of weighted lure — the fly — selected. Right now, the shinier ones are more successful than the feathered ones, but I confirm that both are easy to snag on a rock. All this action allows me to quickly hone my skill, getting ready to graduate to tussles with rarer and bigger cohos, and, if I'm lucky, steelhead or Chinook. Of course, "quickly" and "fishing" don't usually go together: this is a sport of patience. Sky tells me the best part of his job is watching anglers grow and develop skills. Seventy percent of his clients are repeat clientele, many flying in from the U.S. and Europe. For fly-fishing enthusiasts, you can't beat this combination of stunning nature, exclusive access, and abundant fish.

We have a snack, pack our rods, and gracefully take off for another location. It's not like the action could possibly be any better elsewhere, but maybe there will be more coho or steelhead to test our skills. Ocean-living steelhead trout are the glory fish around here, known as the "fish of a thousand casts." Difficult to catch and elusive, they live up to ten years and, unlike salmon, return to the same streams to spawn *multiple* times in their lifetime. High season runs September to early November, and even if the steelhead aren't about, seeing the dramatic snow-tipped Skeena Mountains from the air is a bucket-list-worthy thrill unto itself.

This time we land on a more exposed beach, adjacent to a wide, milky river with an altogether different landscape, running beneath a forest-carpeted mountain. Thousands of old logs are washed up on the shores behind us, and fresh bear prints wander across the sand. Wearing gaiters, I wade waist-deep into the icy waters and roll cast, watching my fly drift with the current. Unlike at the "cast and catch" spot before, here it takes time to hook a fish. This time I must be patient, and hope that my patience is rewarded.

Reader, it was *huge*. Massive! A *blue whale* of a coho. Fifteen, no twenty, no forty pounds! It could have fed a village, I swear. We're back at Northern Escape Mountain Lodge, sharing fishy tales over a scrumptious gourmet dinner paired with fine B.C. wine. The size of the catch increases with every telling. We toast to a remarkable part of the world. With toys like helicopters, jet boats, and e-mountain bikes on the itinerary, this is the bucket-list way to experience it. Heli-*yeah*!

THE GHOST TOWNS OF NORTHERN B.C.

Northern Escape Mountain Lodge arranges jet-boat and heli-tours to several extraordinary ghost towns. Kitsault resembles a typical small coastal community: wooden houses lining neat asphalt lanes, two large recreation centres, a few apartment buildings, a community centre, a medical clinic, a library, and a shopping mall. The grass is cut, the street lamps stand tall, and upon landing in a parking lot, a sign welcomes us to *Kitsault: Heaven on Earth*. One thing is jarringly absent: people. Abandoned when the price of molybdenum crashed in the 1980s, the entire ghost town was bought on auction by a U.S. millionaire, and his workers continue to maintain it as a snapshot of nostalgia and loss. Not far away, the town of Anyox once serviced the largest copper mine in the British Empire. Today it represents a more traditional ghost-town experience, all rust and ruins. Visitors can explore the concrete bones of a dam, flaking buildings, chimney stacks, and houses.

SKI THE TORCH PARADE

Night skiing on New Year's Eve

⊙ Sun Peaks Resort
🔗 canadianbucketlist.com/torchparade

REGARDLESS OF HOW WE APPROACH IT, LIFE IS ABOUT
moments: those precious, unique, and exhilarating seconds that evolve
into the stories that define us. I'm having just such a *moment* on a dark
ski hill, in formation with two hundred others, ready to light up flares.
It's New Year's Eve at Sun Peaks Resort, Canada's second-largest ski

destination. An Olympic legend, former senator, and local pioneer walks our lines, a general inspecting her troops.

"Hold your flare low, go slow, and keep your distance," commands Nancy Greene Raine. Thousands of people have gathered in the village below, bolstered by thumping dance music and festive lights. Kids are waving Glow Sticks.

British Columbia has over eighty-five ski resorts, offering diverse terrain and sitting on a spectrum of hotels, shopping, restaurants, nightlife, and festivals. Some have this and others have that, but Sun Peaks appears to have it all. About a four-and-a-half-hour drive from Vancouver and forty-five minutes from Kamloops, the resort has become a vibrant community, enjoying sixteen square kilometres of skiable terrain, with 137 epic runs serviced by thirteen chairs. The village is modest, with no major hotel or shopping chains, and fantastic dining and accommodation options right off the slopes. It's particularly family-friendly, and with six metres of annual snow and two thousand hours of sunshine, conditions are reliably excellent. Lineups are manageable even on the busiest days, and you can walk through the village in just a few minutes. Despite its vast terrain and increasing international appeal, Sun Peaks still feels like a secret — the snow for those in the know. For New Year's, those in the know register early for the annual Torchlight Parade.

Over dinner at the homely Voyageur Bistro, a short stroll from our comfortable room at the Sun Peaks Grand, a concerned friend turns to me. "Wait, you're going to ski a blue, at night, with an open flame? Esrock, can you even ski?"

It's a valid point. I've only recently ditched my snowboard, learning to ski alongside my kids after realizing that my knees are rusting, and nobody over fifty should be snowboarding anyway. I've heard of festive torchlight runs on other hills, but those are limited to instructors and staff. At Sun Peaks, anyone sixteen and older can sign up for the New Year's Eve Torchlight Parade, presuming they can navigate a blue run, and not roast themselves in a wipeout. I'm not entirely convinced I can do either, but General Nancy inspires confidence.

"There were only ten permanent residents when Al and I moved here," says Nancy, Sun Peaks' Ski Director and Canada's Sportswoman of the Twentieth Century. She is the passionate matriarch of this growing mountain community, where the permanent population of 1,400 continues to rise. Her husband, Al, is the long-serving mayor, and kids take a ski lift to their school at the top of the hill. I once tried to keep up with Nancy on my snowboard, and it was like chasing a Ferrari on a push-bike. It was Nancy who got me up on skis for the first time (she told me I wouldn't fall, and I didn't), but skiing at night with a lit flare is a long way from the bunny hill.

Moonlight batters through the clouds as we ascend on the high-speed Sundance Express, casting a pale glow across the frosted glades. Volunteers with lanterns help us get to our starting point, where we assemble into four lines and receive bamboo poles with attached flares. Everything is timed to perfection. We're given the go-ahead, and Nancy leads the way. We spark our flares with a flint and we begin our torchlight descent, taking wide S-curves amidst elated hollers and yells. It's a jaw-dropping spectacle to witness from the village. From the back of the formation, it looks like we're floating down an exploding volcano, to the crackling sounds of fire and ice. Having pursued my bucket list in nearly 120 countries and across every province and territory in Canada, trust me when I say this *moment* is as good as it gets.

Crowds cheer our arrival as we approach the village. We halt near the bottom, flares still lit, and begin a familiar countdown: ten, nine, eight … At zero, we simultaneously extinguish our flares in the snow, and the first massive firework explodes above our heads. It's a dazzling

WESTERN CANADA'S BEST SKI RESORTS

Whistler Blackcomb, Whistler, B.C.: Eight thousand acres of terrain across two massive mountains, coupled with a world-class village and dynamic off-slope attractions.

Lake Louise Ski Resort, Lake Louise, Alberta: Located in Banff National Park, known for epic mountain views, excellent backcountry, and one of the longest ski seasons on the continent.

Sun Peaks Resort, Sun Peaks, B.C.: Huge terrain, incredible glades, a manageable pedestrian-only village right off the slopes, plenty of sunshine, and a welcoming family-friendly atmosphere.

Revelstoke Mountain Resort, Revelstoke, B.C.: The longest vertical drop in North America, with ample powder, challenging backcountry, sweet glades, and excellent accommodation at the base.

RED Mountain Ski Resort, Rossland, B.C.: Uniquely community owned, RED is a true skier's mountain, with huge amounts of snowfall, few crowds, and the fantastic Josie boutique hotel at the base.

Fernie Alpine Resort, Fernie, B.C.: Legendary bowls, tons of gullies, sweet glades, and a laid-back atmosphere among stunning mountain views and a historic mountain town.

SilverStar Mountain Resort, Vernon, B.C.: The third largest ski resort in B.C. delivers champagne powder in the Monashee Mountains, as well as a colourful Victorian-inspired and family-friendly pedestrian village.

Panorama Mountain Resort, Panorama, B.C.: Gorgeous views, a compact family-friendly village, tremendous runs, and a Monster X Snowcat to access the legendary Taynton Bowl.

BRITISH COLUMBIA

display of light in the darkness, an expression of hope for the year to come. Up to this point, my most memorable New Year's Eve was outside the House of Wonders in Zanzibar. Sydney Harbour, Trafalgar Square, and Copacabana Beach were fun, but way too crowded. No global landmark can possibly compare to alpine skiing at night with lit flares under the direction of an Olympic legend, greeted by cheering crowds and massive fireworks.

In another stroke of planning genius, it's all over by 9:00 p.m., allowing families to relish the celebration and choose whether the kids can hang on to New Year's. My young kids just make it, thanks to hot chocolate and great friends. In time, they too will learn that it's all about these special *moments*, wherever you happen to find them.

CHEERS TO THE ALE TRAIL

Stops for hops

⚲ Around B.C.
⬦ canadianbucketlist.com/beer

THERE IS SIMPLY NO EXCUSE TO DRINK SWILL, ESPECIALLY IN British Columbia. Since the province launched Canada's first microbrewery back in 1982, the craft-beer scene has exploded like luscious hops on the palate, with over two hundred craft breweries blossoming throughout the province. Credit the fresh mountain water, innovative brewers, an insatiable public thirst, and access to outstanding regional hops and malts. Launched in 2016, the B.C. Ale Trail (bcaletrail.ca) offers self-guided itineraries to breweries around the province. Meanwhile Vancouver Brewery Tours and others offer popular guided visits to the best and most diverse local breweries in the city, allowing you to learn all about the beer-making process, taste plenty of beer, and get shuttled around safely. Raise your IPA, Gose, porter, stout, hazy IPA, Pilsner, lager, ESB, sour, saison, amber, or pale ale to say: cheers!

BRITISH COLUMBIA

ALBERTA

EXPERIENCE THE STAMPEDE

Leave your hat on

📍 Calgary

🔗 canadianbucketlist.com/stampede

IT MEANS MANY THINGS TO MANY PEOPLE, BUT THERE'S NO denying the Calgary Stampede — that ten-day Cowtown spectacle — is something to experience before you die. For those who have been, or locals who live it, no explanation is necessary. For the rest of you, take it from a city slicker who came to love his inner yahoo and wear his white hat, buckle, and boots with pride.

The annual festival attracts millions of people, from Western Canada and beyond. Among them are young party animals, herded through gates into wild nights at Cowboys, Nashville North, and other venues around town. They see the Stampede as an excuse to drink beer, dance on sticky floors, flirt (in boots), perhaps go home with someone, wake up, hate themselves, and repeat it all the following day. Strangely enough, older celebrants don't stray too far from the above, perhaps preferring smaller venues such as Ranchman's or music festivals like the Roundup. This is one of the world's biggest parties, if you're into that sort of thing, which the Stampede is more than willing to provide you an excuse to be.

Of course, the Stampede is also the world's richest rodeo. Before I understood exactly what the rodeo is, how it works, and who's behind it, I always rooted for the bulls and horses. I'd yell at my TV set: "Trample that guy in the mud!" I'm sure I'm not alone, but it all changed when I decided to actually see what was going on for myself. Interviewing riders, judges, farmers, and vets, I found myself busting one rodeo myth after the next. No, the testicles of the animals are not strung up to make them buck. No, rodeo animals don't usually get hurt (and they receive the best possible medical attention when they do). Yes, riders have the utmost respect for the animals, and they bear the brunt of the injuries. No, the animals are never overworked, but they are bred for their bucking ability, and they live out their days like champions in the pasture. And yes, it's dangerous, as even a mechanical bull will snap your wrist. It's always difficult to lift a veil of assumptions, but having finally learned

TIPS FOR THE STAMPEDE

1. If you don't have boots, get a pair at the Alberta Boot Company, which has been furnishing cowboys and their accountants for more than thirty years. That pain you feel breaking them in makes you a better person.
2. Pick up the traditional Calgary White Hat at Smithbilt, official hat maker for the event, and for the stars. Do not take it off, even when you sleep.
3. Never say "Yeehaw." It's "Yahoo." Remember that, or face a world of shame.
4. Line up for free bacon pancakes and festive chit-chat each morning at Fluor Rope Square. Do not make fun of the rodeo clowns.
5. Ride the abnormally fast Ferris wheel, pet an animal, visit the exhibitions, watch a miniature horse show, eat lunch in the Big Four Roadhouse, gear up for the rodeo.
6. Always stick around for the Grandstand Show and fireworks.
7. Interact with local wildlife at Cowboys, Nashville North, or Ranchman's.

more about the rodeo, I see a timeless confrontation between man and beast, in fierce but relatively harmless battle, catering to and supported by the very people who work with animals in their daily lives. Animal rights activists may still want to string me up by my testicles, but I'll say this: go check out the rodeo, meet the people, see the animals, and form an educated opinion.

Finally, there's Cowtown itself: Calgary. During Stampede, you'll find an unmistakable community permeating everything: the free pancake breakfasts, the parades, the exhibitions. Look at the dedication on the faces of the Young Canadians performing under the stars. Greet smiling volunteers who make the event tick, taking unpaid leave from work in order to do so.

HAVE YOURSELF A BALL

Bottlescrew Bill's Pub in Calgary has served its infamous prairie oysters for decades, part of a boisterous Testicle Festival that takes place during the annual Stampede. These oysters are as removed from seafood as catnip from a banjo, but they do carry flavour surprisingly well. Buses of tourists show up specifically to sample them, and patrons will consume up to one hundred kilograms of cajones over the ten days. Organ meat tends to taste like organ meat, and while I grew up eating chopped liver, I'm not ordering seconds.

"Any time you can give back to the community, and help them out a little bit, you get something out of it," TV's legendary "Mantracker," Terry Grant, tells me. He's been a volunteer at the Stampede for years.

During my second Stampede, I was hell-bent on breaking in a pair of boots, and never left the hotel without my white hat. I'd only ever dressed like a cowboy at Halloween parties, but now I could slot right in. Boots make me stand taller, puffing out my chest. The cowboy still holds power in our modern age. Certainly, there are those who avoid the Stampede like a warm pile of cow droppings, but there's no denying the sheer energy that shakes up the city. Boots and hats are everywhere, kids have cotton-candy grins, the midway is buzzing. Like many items on the Canadian bucket list, the Stampede is a saddle that will fit some better than others. But as a true Canadian celebration of western roots and community spirit, you can't miss it.

SKI IN A UNESCO WORLD HERITAGE SITE

Excuse us, we need to powder our views

📍 Banff National Park

🔗 canadianbucketlist.com/skibig3

SOME OF THE WORLD HERITAGE SITES I'VE VISITED AROUND the globe consist of little more than historical rubble. Others are miss-them-if-you-blink-really-that-was-it? And some, like Banff National Park, are just so staggering they belong in another category altogether.

In any season, the Canadian Rockies are the picture postcard of Canada, with a vast carpet of forest, water, glacier, and mountain waiting to drop your jaw. It took a mad sort of genius, and considerable Canadian elbow grease, to set up three different ski resorts inside Banff National Park: Lake Louise, Sunshine, and Norquay. Come winter, you can literally slide down the wilderness that surrounds you. Lake Louise, the third-biggest ski resort in Canada, is View Central. Enjoying the resort's runs, I often had to stop and plop my butt in the snow simply to admire the vista. I was determined to hit every lift in one day, which I did, and I was not disappointed. Here is a mountain for people who love mountains: million-dollar views, not million-dollar condos.

Closer to Banff town centre is Sunshine Village, a smaller resort famed for its champagne powder. Staying at the Sunshine Mountain Lodge, Banff's only ski-in, ski-out boutique lodge, it's easy enough to awake each morning to catch "first chair" and reap the rewards. Sunshine has the kind of snow that makes your skis smile. This from a guy who grew up in Africa, who first saw snow as a six-year-old during a freak storm in Johannesburg, and was told to hide under his school desk in case it was ash from nuclear fallout. True story, but I digress.

With many ski resorts in Western Canada offering world-class conditions without even trying, what's the big deal about a UNESCO designation? Abundant wildlife? It's highly unlikely that you will ski among moose and elk (although one instructor told me his girlfriend saw a wolverine during a run). Sunshine, Norquay, and Lake Louise — the Big Three, as they co-market themselves — look like typical resorts, with lifts and quads and young Australians sweeping chairs in exchange for a season pass. There are après-ski bars serving craft beer and knee-high plates of nachos. So how is this different, you may ask? It could be the views from the chairs at Lake Louise. It could be the snow at Sunshine. It could be the homeyness of Norquay. It could even be the proximity of iconic and grand

WESTERN CANADA'S UNESCO WORLD HERITAGE SITES

As of this writing, Western Canada has seven of Canada's UNESCO World Heritage Sites, mostly in Alberta. Several more await on UNESCO's Tentative List, as more natural and cultural wonders become recognized and protected for their global cultural, historical, and natural significance.

SG̲ang Gwaay, B.C.: Consisting of large cedar longhouses, mortuary, and memorial totem poles, this site preserves a nineteenth-century village of the Haida people.

Canadian Rocky Mountain Parks, Alberta: Encompassing seven national parks and protected for exceptional natural beauty as well as the Burgess Shale formation, this is one of the world's most important Cambrian fossil sites.

Dinosaur Provincial Park, Alberta: Fossils of every known group of Cretaceous dinosaurs have been found in this park, located in the striking Badlands.

Head-Smashed-In Buffalo Jump, Alberta: A well-preserved and rare example of a buffalo jump, the traditional hunting method of the Plains peoples for over six millennia.

Waterton-Glacier International Peace Park, Alberta: Straddling the Continental Divide and celebrated for outstanding scenic beauty, this unique geographical spot is home to an unusually high number of plant and animal species.

Writing-on-Stone/Áísínai'pi, Alberta: Sacred to the Niitsítapi people, this site contains the greatest concentration of rock art on the North American Great Plains.

Wood Buffalo National Park, Northwest Territories/Alberta: The world's largest inland delta is home to the continent's largest population of wild bison, as well as the breeding ground for the endangered whooping crane.

Canadian hotels: Fairmont Banff Springs and Fairmont Château Lake Louise. On investigation, I can confirm it's all of the above, wrapped in a shell of deep respect for a stunning environment — safe, protected, but available to be enjoyed.

HUNT FOR DINOSAURS

Fossil beds for the ages

📍 Dinsosaur Provincial Park
🔗 canadianbucketlist.com/dinosaur

IN THE LAND WHERE THE MIGHTY TYRANNOSAURUS REX
roared, we honour the beaver. Oh, what irony that the fiercest creatures
to ever roam the planet have been unearthed, literally, in Canada. T. rex
would have used beavers as tennis balls — assuming dinosaurs played
tennis or coexisted with beavers. Regardless, the theropod's old bones,
unearthed alongside many others in southern Alberta's Badlands,
contribute significantly to the world's richest fossil bed.

Like most young boys, I was fascinated by dinosaurs, reciting their
long-winded-saurus names and taking extra time to look at today's

tiny lizards, wondering where it all went wrong. Or, given the rise of us mammals, right. Unfortunately, by the time I arrived at Dinosaur Provincial Park, I was just another jaded adult too consumed by maturity to appreciate the fact that I had just plucked a seventy-million-year-old dinosaur bone directly from the ground. The kids around me, however, went berserk.

All it takes is a little imagination. Seventy-five million years ago, the Red Deer River valley was as lush and tropical as Central America. Huge beasts roamed about, looking very much like giant lizards, or birds, or museum skeletons, depending on which theory you choose to believe in.

When the dinosaurs woke up to the Worst Day Ever and promptly died, their bones settled on the riverbed, covered by soft sandstone and mudstone, and were all but forgotten until the 1800s. At this point, the fiercest creatures on earth — humans — now wore funny hats. During the last ice age, a glacier had removed the top level of dirt, exposing hundreds of bones from more than forty types of dinosaurs, including Tyrannosauridae, Hypsilophodontidae, and Ankylosauria (you know, the ones with thick ankles). Today, this UNESCO World Heritage Site is more than just Dinosaur Central. Sure, the visitor centre and interpretation drives are interesting, and you can drive a couple of hours to the Royal Tyrrell Museum of Palaeontology in Drumheller to see what the fossils look like cleaned up and bolted together. But it's the landscape itself that struck me, dare I say it, like a meteor.

The Badlands are so called because the soil makes this land terrible for farming but wonderful for filming science fiction. Cracked grey earth resembling the skin of an elephant is tightly wrapped around phallic rocks called hoodoos. Rattlesnakes shake among the riverside cottonwoods, while the much smaller descendants of dinosaurs fly overhead or bask in the sun. Taking it all in, it's hard not to appreciate the scale of our planet's history, and the palaeontological riches of Alberta.

ON THE BUCKET LIST: DR. PHILIP J. CURRIE

The world's foremost dinosaur expert (Sam Neill's character in Jurassic Park *was partially based on Dr. Currie) digs into the bucket list:*

The Milk River Canyon north of the American border is Alberta's deepest canyon and is also in the most sparsely populated region in the southern half of the province. The unhindered view of prairie grasslands is augmented by a great bowl-like depression that slopes down toward the canyon, offering a spectacular view of the mysterious Sweetgrass Hills on the south side of the border. The Badlands have produced some of the most interesting fossils from the province, including embryonic duck-billed dinosaurs within eggs and a superbly preserved skeleton of the ancestor of Tyrannosaurus rex!

— Dr. Philip J. Currie, world-renowned palaeontologist,
co-founder of the Royal Tyrrell Museum of Palaeontology

A couple of years later, I find myself extracting an articulated bone from a fossil bed cut into a steep cliff, an hour outside Grande Prairie. I am almost a thousand kilometres north of the Badlands, at the site of yet another remarkable discovery. Here, among oil and gas platforms, lies one of the world's *next*-richest fossil beds, as palaeontologists from around the globe work each summer in sun and rain to extract one fossil after another. One of the world's most famous dinosaur experts, Canada's own Dr. Philip J. Currie, spearheaded the charge, complete with a twenty-six-million-dollar namesake museum to house these newfound treasures unearthed from the area. Oil and gas have made Alberta Canada's richest province. Yet its earth continues to yield riches that give us profound insight into the past. Whether you're into history, museums, or just unusual scenery, join the hunt for dinosaurs in Alberta. At least before a meteor comes out of nowhere, causes a deep impact, blocks out the sun, wipes out life, and forces you, inconveniently, to wait another seventy million years for the opportunity.

HIKE THE SKY

Adventures above the treeline

📍 Jasper National Park
🔗 canadianbucketlist.com/skyline

WIDELY REGARDED AS THE BEST HIKE IN THE ROCKIES, OVER half of Jasper National Park's forty-four-kilometre Skyline Trail is above the treeline. Expect spectacular views as you cut across ridges that overlook crystal lakes, alpine meadows, and Tolkien-esque valleys. Be aware that hiking this high up also means greater exposure to the

SOMEWHERE, OUT THERE …

Wildlife is abundant in Jasper and Banff National Parks, but so is space. The two national parks cover a staggering 17,869 square kilometres, populated by cautious animals that trod on trapper and hunting lists for generations. There are only about three hundred black and grizzly bears roaming both parks, and you'd have to be both lucky and horribly unlucky to encounter one. The vast majority of bear encounters are fleeting and harmless, but rare bear attacks do make the news (as one did in the backcountry of Banff in late 2023). Along with moose, wapiti — which Europeans call moose and we call elk — wolverines, wolves, mountain goats, and other furry wonders, bears typically want nothing to do with us. When it comes to wildlife in the Rockies, it's best to lower your expectations with the hope of being pleasantly surprised.

elements, particularly along the ridge, where strong wind and whipping rain can make life particularly miserable for trekkers. When in doubt, channel Frodo … he always kept going.

Depending on your level of fitness and sense of purpose, the Skyline Trail can be completed in anywhere from two to six days, and there are well-serviced campsites along the way. If you're lucky, you might see some of the animals that roam the high valleys looking for food, such as wolves, grizzly bears, and mountain lions. You'll feel even luckier if you're carrying bear spray.

Due to the unpredictable weather, invest in quality gear, including a camping stove, since no fires are allowed on the trail. Tour companies in Jasper offer a shuttle service between the trailheads of Maligne Canyon and Maligne Lake, with most hikers choosing to start at the lake, avoiding a nasty early ascent. As this is one of the best-known hikes in the Rockies, booking ahead is essential.

RV THE ICEFIELDS PARKWAY

It's not what you do, it's who you do it with

📍 Lake Louise/Jasper

🔗 canadianbucketlist.com/icefields

THE FIRST TIME I HAULED A BACKPACK AROUND THE WORLD, I had a wonderful sensation of independence. Everything I needed was right there: clothes, toiletries, books, cash, a sense of adventure. My daily challenge was deciding where to sleep and use the toilet. The first time I went on an RV adventure, I felt that familiar gush

WESTERN CANADA'S BUCKET-LIST RV DESTINATIONS

- ➤ Porteau Cove Provincial Park, B.C.
- ➤ Rathtrevor Beach Provincial Park, B.C.
- ➤ The Similkameen Valley, B.C.
- ➤ Wells Gray Provincial Park, B.C.
- ➤ Mount Robson Provincial Park, B.C.
- ➤ Yoho National Park, B.C.
- ➤ Banff National Park, Alberta
- ➤ Jasper National Park, Alberta
- ➤ Drumheller and the Badlands, Alberta
- ➤ Bow Valley Provincial Park, Alberta
- ➤ Waterton Lakes National Park, Alberta
- ➤ Peter Lougheed Provincial Park, Alberta

of independence, only the daily challenges were flushed away with the black water.

RV sales were steadily increasing before the Covid-19 pandemic, and exploded during it. A whole new demographic of millennials and Gen-Xers discovered the leisure and pleasure of taking comforts on the road with you, joining boomers and empty nesters who have known all along.

According to Go RVing, the industry's marketing coalition, about 15 percent of Canadian households own an RV. This inspired my dad, my brothers, and me to rent a nine-metre Winnebago for a week's "mancation" to the Rockies. We would become just one of over two million RVs on Canadian roads that summer, the others likely driven by folks with far more experience than us. With a complete kitchen, two television sets, a bedroom, and a bathroom, our RV rattled and rolled its way out of Vancouver, wobbling in the wind with the aerodynamics of a cement brick. I was driving, my brothers were yelling: "Too close to the side!" "Watch the lines!" "You almost hit that car!" Ah yes, just a few hours in and I could feel our mancation easing my stress … right up behind my eyeballs and straight to the back of my throat.

My dad has always been in love with mountains, but since emigrating from South Africa he'd never had the opportunity to see the Rockies. For the full effect, I steered our roadworthy beast to Highway 93 — a.k.a. the Icefields Parkway — a 232-kilometre stretch of road between Lake Louise and Jasper. It is, without a doubt, one of the world's most spectacular drives, a gee-whiz postcard moment awaiting drivers at every turn. The visual impact of the mountains and glaciers that line the highway rivals that of the Himalayas, but, boy, the roads are better and the Rockies are a lot easier to get to. Passing turquoise lakes and glacier-cut mountains, we craned our necks from side to side to capture the view out of the large windows, as if watching a game of tennis. The overall effect, especially for someone who enjoys mountain beauty, can be as rich as a chocolate fondue. "It's too much," I heard my dad reporting to my mom on his phone. "But in a good way."

Rock flour, crushed and carried by glaciers, makes mountain lakes glow in luminous shades of blue and green. We visit Moraine Lake on a postcard-perfect day, getting our photo in front of one of Canada's most popular and sought-after views. By the time we reach Peyto Lake, farther up the highway, our camera batteries need refuelling from the RV's generator. The RV's height, big windows, and ease of movement make it the perfect vehicle from which to gawk at the mountains, if not always to park. Thank you, Parks Canada, for the extra-long parking bays at all the major sites. Parks Canada protects our wilderness, and they park Canada too!

We pop into the Athabasca Glacier, where monster customized four-by-four buses take us directly onto a six-kilometre-long ice floe in the Columbia Icefield. Out on the ice, I scoop up melted water, drinking the taste of nature at its purest.

Bookending the Icefields Parkway are two of Canada's most iconic wilderness areas: Banff and Jasper National Parks. No surprise that we came across a bear chewing berries along the road, or a huge elk stopping traffic in its tracks. During the week, we take the Banff Gondola and the Jasper SkyTram, barbecue steaks in an RV park, play a terrific round of golf at the Jasper Park Lodge, rent Harley-Davidsons to rocket up Mount Edith Cavell, and even swim in the ice-cold waters of a glacial lake. It is, in short, an epic mancation, immersed in true Canadiana. We even manage to keep the rental RV in relatively good shape, although on the last night of our journey we realize that nobody had been paying too much attention to the instructions about how to empty the black water. Push a few buttons, pull a few knobs, and the next thing we know, the tube comes loose and drenches all three brothers. Truth be told, black water looks rather yellow. My dad would have wet himself laughing, but of course we'd already beaten him to it.

I've driven the Icefields Parkway several times since, yet this RV trip stands out. True travel magic is not about what you're doing, it's about whom you're doing it with. Wise words to remember when crossing off any item on your bucket list.

OGLE AT MORAINE LAKE

The most iconic view in the Rockies

📍 Banff National Park

🔗 canadianbucketlist.com/moraine

FIFTEEN MINUTES FROM LAKE LOUISE LIES ONE OF THE most magnificent and iconic views in all of Canada. The jewels of the Rockies gather in one magical spot — dramatic snow-capped peaks, emerald evergreen forest, a turquoise lake, and an easy-to-access lookout point — sparkling together on a crown of natural

ALBERTA

beauty the entire nation wears with pride.

It took less than a decade after its discovery in 1899 for tourists to start arriving at Moraine Lake, which was soon serviced by a tea house, and later tents and log cabins. Today, visitors will find luxury accommodations in the form of the Arthur Erickson–designed Moraine Lake Lodge, which is open each summer. As one of the most popular natural attractions in the country, Moraine Lake had long become overly saturated with vehicles and frustrated visitors each June to October. In 2023, Parks Canada decided it best to close Moraine Lake Road to all personal vehicles, operating a Park and Ride shuttle from the Lake Louise Ski Resort instead. With crowds more manageable, take your time and enjoy it. On a sunny day, with the Valley of the Ten Peaks reflected in the water, you just might think you've died and gone to heaven.

BUCKET-LIST WEDDINGS

My friends Lili and Brian got married above Peyto Lake in Banff National Park. They'd planned their pop-up wedding for Moraine Lake, but heavy summer crowds put the kibosh on that idea. Peyto Lake proved to be just as spectacular. If you have less than twenty guests and apply for a free wedding ceremony application, any couple can pop up and tie the knot against the backdrop of Western Canada's most striking national park.

ALBERTA

STEP OVER THE ROCKIES

Walk off a cliff

⚲ Jasper National Park

🔗 canadianbucketlist.com/skywalk

ALBERTA

THE ROCKY MOUNTAINS AND ICEFIELDS PARKWAY HAVE NO shortage of mind-blowing views. Yet there's always room for more, especially if we can add in the word "knee-shaking." Inspired by the Grand Canyon Skywalk, the same folks behind the Columbia Icefield glacier tours spent twenty-one million dollars building a horseshoe-shaped glass-floor observation deck extending thirty-five metres over and three hundred metres above Jasper National Park's Sunwapta Valley. Opened in 2014, the Columbia Icefield Skywalk is another meaty mouthful of natural beauty in a region that won't stop dishing it out until you explode — or at least unbuckle your belt.

With the environmental blessing of Parks Canada, your experience begins at the Columbia Icefield Glacier Discovery Centre down the road. A shuttle departs every fifteen minutes from existing parking lot facilities, ensuring no additional paradise paving was necessary. The short bus ride is further symbolic since it was a company bus driver who originally conceived the idea of a suspension bridge across the valley. Architects did one better, creating the steel-and-glass structure that places you right into the view itself. First you must walk through six interpretative stations, revealing the natural history, ecology, wildlife, and geology of the area. When you're suitably informed, the giant glass horseshoe awaits.

Glass is a funny thing. Even when it's reinforced, 3.81 inches thick, and capable of withstanding the weight of two Boeing 747s, it still seems woefully inadequate. Especially when you take your first steps off a cliff and see the ground disappear between your feet. Some people just don't do heights — be it bungee jumping or glass platform observation decks. I'd suggest they take the Columbia Icefield Tour while the rest of us walk nervously forward to the apex of the platform. Immediately apparent: the skywalk jiggles slightly when you walk. Engineers designed the platform to withstand metres of heavy snow and sway safely in strong valley winds. Suspended high above the valley floor, you'll eventually be able to tear your eyes (and cameras) away from your feet and look out at Mount Andromeda, the Snow Dome, and its surroundings. You might even spot a bighorn sheep on the valley floor below. Standing on that platform is a bucket-list moment, one that some visitors will want to experience for as long as they can. Others will be more than happy to take a few pictures and return their feet to solid earth.

VISIT AN OASIS OF WILDLIFE

Don't call them buffalo

📍 Elk Island National Park

🔗 canadianbucketlist.com/elkisland

THE BISON, NORTH AMERICA'S LARGEST TERRESTRIAL mammal, once roamed the plains in the millions. Indigenous people hunted the huge beasts for meat and skins, and there was more than enough to go around. The arrival of European hunters, however, quickly took the species to the brink of extinction. Today, wild bison are protected in enclaves of national parks, the most famous and certainly the largest being Wood Buffalo National Park. Far more accessible, and just as significant, is Elk Island National Park, an hour's drive east of Edmonton. The country's only entirely fenced national park, Elk Island is  a haven for free-roaming bison, not to mention elk, deer, moose, and more than 250 species of birds. Here, Canada's largest mammal shares its habitat with Canada's smallest — the pygmy shrew.

By the year 1900, there were as few as 1,500 plains bison remaining. Early conservation efforts saw the establishment of Elk Island in 1906, with several hundred pure-bred plains bison shipped up from Montana. Their numbers rebounded, and the park successfully relocated bison throughout Canada, the United States, and even as far as Russia. Elk Island also contains the most genetically pure wood bison remaining, as the two species have interbred everywhere else. These two breeds are kept separate in the park, with wood bison on the south side of the Yellowhead Highway and plains bison on the north side. On either side, visitors can leave their cars to hike or hit the mountain biking trails in summer, and snowshoe or cross-country ski in winter. On these treks, it's not uncommon to encounter grazing bison herds and other wildlife. Today, there are more than eight hundred bison in the park, the number maintained so as not to overwhelm their sanctuary. Parks Canada's interpretation and conservation efforts are an encouraging sign that bison will remain a wildlife encounter on Western Canada bucket lists for many years to come.

ALBERTA

GO BIG AT THE WEST EDMONTON MALL

Anything you can do we can do bigger

📍 Edmonton

🔗 canadianbucketlist.com/wem

YES, I'M FULLY AWARE HOW THIS LOOKS. HERE'S A BOOK WITH the ultimate things to do in Western Canada before you die, and you just read: visit a mall. It's not even the biggest mall in the world. That honour belongs to — no, wait, someone else just built a bigger one. Yet Canadian malls are a little different. Take Montreal's Underground City. Officially called RÉSO, it's a warren of tunnels beneath twelve square kilometres of downtown Montreal, linking shops, hotels, residential buildings, schools, train and bus stations, offices, and tourists searching for a glimpse of daylight. Calgary has its four-storey CORE, beneath three city blocks and with 160 stores. "Big deal!" yawn our friends in Ontario, where Toronto's Eaton Centre has 330 stores, Brampton's Bramalea City Centre has 342, and Mississauga's Square One a whopping 360 places of commercial worship. In British Columbia, where people can actually step outside in winter, Burnaby's Metropolis at Metrotown trumps them all, with over 400 stores, including a massive Asian supermarket. Yes, Canadians like to shop, and by the looks of it, they like to shop at the same chain stores you'll find at just about every mall in the country.

And then, suddenly, like an unexplained star burning across the retail sky, you get the phenomenon of the West Edmonton Mall. The largest mall in North America, heck the largest mall in the western hemisphere, has over 800 stores, covering 570 square kilometres of retail, more than double the size of B.C.'s Metropolis. There's parking for more than twenty thousand cars, it employs more than twenty thousand people, it receives thirty million visitors a year, and it's Alberta's busiest tourist attraction.

I hear you asking, "Robin, seriously, isn't one mall just a carbon copy of the next? Stores, food court, gadget stores, teenagers in paint-on jeans, glass elevators, confusing maps?"

I thought so, too, until I found myself pulling the trigger of a .44 Magnum revolver, blasting a bottle-cap hole in my paper target at the shooting range — at the West Edmonton Mall. How many malls are accredited as a zoo? How many malls boast one of the world's largest indoor amusement parks, and one of the largest indoor water parks on the planet? At this mall, you can say hello to the sea lion that swims beneath a replica of Señor Columbus's *Santa Maria*, skate on

CAR #1 AND FRIENDS

Edmonton's streetcars went the way of the dodo in 1951, with all but Car #1 sent to the scrap heap of history. After decades of neglect, #1 was lovingly restored for a run across the High Level Bridge to celebrate the city's seventy-fifth anniversary in 1979. Inspired by this event, an Edmonton railway society was formed, and five years later, #1 commenced service at Fort Edmonton Park. Other antique streetcars in despair were rescued and brought to the city, including cars from Osaka, Melbourne, Toronto, and Saskatoon. Service was expanded in the 1990s, and today the Edmonton Radial Railway operates century-old streetcars each summer along former CPR tracks from historic Old Strathcona across the High Level Bridge into downtown Edmonton.

an Olympic-sized hockey rink, and then transplant yourself to New Orleans, Paris, or Beijing at one of three themed areas: Bourbon Street, Europa Boulevard, and Chinatown. Should you get tired of walking around trying to make sense of the thoughtfully provided maps, take a nap in one of the mall's two hotels. Universal Studios is taking an additional forty-five acres with a massive new indoor theme park, part of a $7.1-billion-dollar upgrade at the mall announced in 2023. The world's biggest mall is only getting bigger.

You might expect to find such a mall in Vegas, or perhaps Dubai, which stole the Biggest Mall in the World title before relinquishing it to China, Malaysia, and the Philippines. Asian malls dominate the list of biggest malls, but standing out like a proud beaver among the tigers is our very own West Edmonton Mall.

HIKE OR SKI INTO SKOKI LODGE

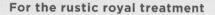

For the rustic royal treatment

⚲ Lake Louise Ski Resort
𝒫 canadianbucketlist.com/skoki

IN 1931, SWISS MOUNTAIN GUIDES AND MEMBERS OF THE Banff Ski Club decided to build Western Canada's first commercial ski lodge. With thousands of kilometres to choose from, they settled on a place called Skoki, selected for its scenic beauty, quality of snow, proximity to a creek, and safety from avalanches. Today, one of the oldest

ALBERTA

and highest backcountry lodges in Canada is located eleven kilometres from the groomed ski slopes of the Lake Louise Ski Resort, and I'm feeling every step of it.

It's my first time on cross-country skis, slipping and sliding forth with surprising ease. A strip of material under each ski, called the skin, grips the snow as I edge my way through pine forest, over frozen lakes, and across windy mountain passes. Every Skoki guest must ski, hike, or snowshoe in, unless you're the Prince and Princess of Wales, in which case Parks Canada will organize a helicopter. Skoki made headlines for attracting the newlywed William and Kate on their Canadian honeymoon. No electricity, no cellphone or Internet coverage, no running water, no paparazzi — Skoki provided a rustic royal break from the media frenzy. It wasn't the first royal connection either: one of the lodge's first guests was one Lady Jean, a lady-in-waiting to Queen Victoria, who visited Skoki with her travel-writer husband, Niall Rankin.

While the Rankins used the outhouse like regular guests, William and Kate had a specially built bathroom constructed for their visit, which was hastily destroyed afterward, lest regular guests get any modern ideas.

Skoki strives to be as authentic a backcountry experience today as it was in the 1930s. That means candles, blankets, and late-night stumbles to the outhouse during blizzards. It's one of the best winter adventures in North America, with an emphasis on adventure. You'll know this as you make your way up Deception Pass, a steep uphill trail that keeps going, and going, and going. By the time I arrive at the lodge, covered in sweat and snow from too many downhill tumbles, the fireplace is surrounded by guests enjoying hot homemade soup. Skoki accommodates up to twenty-two guests, and we each feel we deserve our place on one of the sink-in couches. Among the guests are two Norwegians, a ski club from Manitoba, a couple returning for the ninth time from the Northwest Territories, a birthday party, and a couple on their second honeymoon (staying in the Honeymoon cabin, of course). Will and Kate, who signed the guest book like everyone else, preferred the Riverside cabin, close to the creek. I offload my gear in a cabin called Wolverine, named for the wolverine that got stuck in it and almost tore it to shreds. While Skoki's original builders took refuge in a special bear-safe tree, the bears, cougars, and wolves that roam Banff National Park nowadays keep their distance. The most bothersome creatures appear to be pine martens, porcupines, and exhausted travel writers.

Skoki itself is the launch pad for hiking and skiing trails, which most guests explore on their second day. Two-night stays are typical, giving you just about enough time to recover from the eleven-kilometre trek in order to do it all over again. Nobody can expect to lose much weight, however. The chef and staff somehow prepare gourmet meals, such as coconut-crusted Alaskan halibut, marinated tenderloin served with candied yams, avocado Caesar salad, and fresh homemade bread. That everything is

packed in by snowmobile (horses in summer) and prepared using propane stoves makes it all the more impressive — and appreciated.

The discussion by the fire revolves mostly around Skoki's beauty, history, and legacy. One couple sifts through the guest books until they find the last time they signed it, in 1974. Another guest plays the piano, which was helicoptered in sometime in the early 1980s. I read an old book about western Canadian outlaws, play with the resident dogs, and let the fresh air and exercise sink into my pores. On my final night, the moon is so full I can read without a headlamp. Miles away from anything, protected by a world of mountains, forest, and snow, Skoki is the perfect escape, for royals, and the rest of us too.

VISIT A SITE FOR ALL EYES

Jasper's scenic star

📍 Jasper National Park
🔗 canadianbucketlist.com/maligne

THE ROCKIES ROCK IN ALL SEASONS, WHICH IS YOU YOU can't go wrong whenever you choose to visit them. If it's warm and sunny, you hit the hikes. If it's cold and snowy, you ski the slopes. Or, in the case of Maligne Canyon, explore the ice. Despite the shadowy roots of its name (from the old French word for "evil"), Maligne is

Jasper National Park's top-rated attraction. In the summer months, a river barrels through crevices in the limestone canyon, some as deep as fifty metres. This rush of water is best viewed from the well-trodden footpath and a series of six bridges, accessible via an easy two-hour round-trip walk with the welcome refreshment of pure glacier waterfall spray. Exit, as always, through the gift shop.

In winter, the gushing water freezes on the canyon floor, ideal for a guided ice-walk both alongside and through the canyon. Tour operators provide the cleats, headlamp, and interpretation of the canyon's unique topography (it sits above the largest karst cave system in North America). Candle-wax-like ice spikes cover the rocks. Walking among the crystals of the canyon's flash-frozen waterfalls never fails to impress, nor does the sight of water still flowing beneath the ice in some sections. Ice chutes create natural slides, which are particularly popular with the kids. They might want to break off some ice for an all-natural glacial ice lolly — there's plenty to go around — and unlike stalactites, it won't take a thousand years to grow them back. Whether you're chasing raging torrents, sparkling ice, or just the chance to immerse yourself in the beauty of one of Canada's most famous national parks, Maligne Canyon is a bucket-list item for all seasons.

MIST OPPORTUNITIES

Mountains mean waterfalls, and waterfalls mean bucket-list views, mist sprays, and perhaps a swim. Here's a roundup of the best in Western Canada:

Helmcken Falls (B.C.): Located in Wells Gray Provincial Park, Helmcken is an impressive cascade in summer, and even more so in winter, when the water spray at the bottom of the falls freezes, creating a massive ice cone up to fifty metres tall.

Athabasca Falls (Alberta): One of Jasper National Park's most popular attractions, Athabasca Falls makes up for a short twenty-three-metre drop with the fiercest volume in the Rockies. Various paved trails and wheelchair-accessible viewing platforms allow everyone to hear the roar.

Takakkaw Falls (B.C.): Thundering with glacier runoff each summer, Takakkaw (which translates roughly as "magnificent" in Cree) drops 384 metres in total. It's easy to access from mid-June to mid-October with a mostly paved walkway to the base.

Cameron Falls (Alberta): Located inside Waterton Lakes National Park and accessed via an easy trail, this popular year-round attraction has angled bedrock causing the water to stream in different patterns.

Shannon Falls (B.C.): Just before Squamish off the Sea to Sky Highway, follow a popular hiking trail through the dense forest and get rewarded with an impressive cascade that drops over 335 metres.

Elbow Falls (Alberta): About a thirty-five-minute drive from Calgary, you'll find an easy, 0.8-kilometre paved trail outside of Bragg Creek, leading to the falls bursting over a rocky ledge. Accessible year-round, there's a handy recreational area and additional hiking trails.

BOARD THE ROCKY MOUNTAINEER

A bucket-list train journey

⚲ Vancouver to Jasper
🔗 canadianbucketlist.com/rockymountaineer

ALL ABOARD FOR ONE OF THE WORLD'S GREAT TRAIN experiences. I'm not talking about the time I spent thirty-eight hours in a cabin with slaughtered chickens in Zambia, with deafening music blasting through the cobwebbed, distorted speakers. Neither do I refer to the Trans-Siberian Railway, which crosses thousands of kilometres of pretty much nothing. No, the Rocky Mountaineer is an altogether more genteel affair, smothered in five-star service, tasty libations, and views of the Canadian Rockies in all their splendour. Running on four routes going both east and west, the Rocky Mountaineer is North America's largest private rail service. *National Geographic* has called it one of the World's Greatest Trips, and *Condé Nast Traveler* listed it among the Top 5 Trains in the World.

I hopped on board at the station in Vancouver for a two-day journey up to Banff.

Important to note: you don't sleep on the Rocky Mountaineer. The thousand-kilometre journey takes place during daylight so you can enjoy the views, with passengers staying overnight at the company's own hotel in Kamloops. Guests either choose Silverleaf service with single-level glass-dome coaches or the Goldleaf category that includes a two-level domed coach. Both offer panoramic views, drinks service, and a helpful, unnervingly cheery attendant pointing out places of interest along the route. On the way out of B.C. we pass over Hell's Gate, the narrowest point of the Fraser River, and spot a bear walking across the tracks behind us. We enter the engineering marvel of the Spiral Tunnels and are halfway through a game of cards when Mount Robson, the highest mountain in the Rockies, comes into view. That deserves another Caesar.

There's an excellent gourmet meal service and optional activities, such as wine-tasting, to put you nicely in the groove of the rocking train. Of course, like many of life's great luxuries, the comfort comes with a price tag. The trip is ideal for Vancouver–Alaska cruise shippers extending their journey, seniors, or anyone looking for a little bit of romance. Recalling the time I paid ten dollars for an attendant's Snickers bar in Croatia, the only food available for eighteen hours, I can relax knowing that the Rocky Mountaineer is all about the journey, not the destination. If only all journeys were quite as civilized.

ENJOY A SOAK

On the subject of treating oneself, thermal activity in Western Canada has gifted the region with a selection of outstanding hot springs. Some are rugged and surrounded by forests, while others are more upscale, surrounded by golf courses and fine hotels. All offer therapeutic benefits for the mind, body, and soul. Here are ten of the best:

1. Banff Upper Hot Springs, Alberta
2. Liard River Hot Springs, B.C.
3. Kananaskis Nordic Spa, Alberta
4. Harrison Hot Springs, B.C.
5. Miette Hot Springs, Alberta
6. Ainsworth Hot Springs, B.C.
7. Radium Hot Springs, B.C.
8. Hot Springs Cove, B.C.
9. Fairmont Hot Springs, B.C.
10. Halcyon Hot Springs, B.C.

GIDDY-UP WITH A RANCH VACATION

Lasso your inner cowboy

⊗ Medicine Hat
𝒸 canadianbucketlist.com/ranch

COWBOYS DATE BACK TO THE 1700S, THE NAME BEING A direct translation of the Spanish *"vaquero,"* a person who managed cattle by horseback. Cattle drives, averaging around three thousand head, were managed by just ten men or fewer, each with several horses, battling the elements to literally drive meat to the market. The cowboy, often poorly paid, uneducated, and low on the social ladder, had many tasks to perform. These included rounding up the cattle; sorting, securing, and protecting herds from thieves and wild animals; breaking in horses; and birthing and nursing sick animals. The hazardous, strenuous nature of the work created a breed of hardened men, as well as terrific fodder for romance novels eagerly snapped up by urban readers fascinated by the call of the Wild West.

Despite Hollywood's portrayal, there were relatively few violent confrontations with Native Americans. Instead, most Indigenous chiefs were paid in cattle or cash for permission to drive cattle through their lands. Another aspect glossed over in the folklore is that, according to the U.S. census of the time, 30 percent of all cowboys were of African or Mexican ancestry. Giddy-up, amigo! When railways replaced cattle drives, modern cowboys began to work on ranches and show off their skills at competitive rodeos. An alluring myth took hold, and it attracts curious bucket listers to this day.

There are several working ranches in Alberta where you can trade your shoes for boots — roll up, pack in, relax, recharge, or volunteer to help with the chores. My introduction to ranch vacations was with the late, great Bill Moynihan, whose family ranch in the rolling Porcupine Hills welcomed guests to roll up steers, patrol for wild animals, and feed the cattle. Bill's moustache looked like an army guarding his upper lip, and he correctly assessed me as a regular cowpoke with the physical fortitude of a Jenga tower. He chose me a horse, and off we rode to my first roundup. Bill lassoed a young calf and I helped tag it on the ear, nervous that its six-hundred-kilogram mom seemed endearingly protective. I fed the heifers grain and dispensed hay from an industrial tractor. While I barely managed to heave a bale of hay to the shed, Bill walked past me carrying two on each hand. When the zombies attack, find a guy like Bill.

Ranchers have a deep appreciation and respect for the animals and the land that provide their livelihood. They also like to have fun. When Bill taught me how to lasso, the only thing I succeeded in lassoing was my face. City slickers are always good for a laugh around the firepit. The following day, we saddled up to ride to the property fence, making sure nothing was damaged while looking for signs of predators. A strong, icy wind blew across the foothills.

"The biggest thing you can do in life is pass on the thing you love to somebody else," Bill said. He was not a man of many words, but cowboys don't have to be.

Bill Moynihan passed away at the age of eighty-one, and his family ranch no longer offers vacations. Fortunately, there are alternatives, like the thirty-four-thousand-acre Bar Diamond Guest Ranch north of Medicine Hat, and Diane and Bear Baker's Wildhorse Ranch close to Rocky Mountain House.

The word "dude" technically refers to someone who doesn't know cowboy culture but pretends otherwise — "all hat and no cattle." A dude like, say, me. Yet hospitality on a ranch vacation is warm and genuine, and the values of the modern-day cowboy are alive and well. Rest easy, pardner, ranch life remains as real and rewarding as the cowboy myth that continues to promote it.

TRAIL RIDE TO ALLENBY PASS

See somebody about a horse

⌖ Banff National Park
🔗 canadianbucketlist.com/allenbypass

WITH ALL DUE RESPECT TO ROCK-STAR ATTRACTIONS LIKE LAKE
Louise and Moraine Lake, if you truly want to feel the Rockies in your
bones, you'll need to get on a saddle. Specifically, the saddle of a horse
that departs Banff Trail Riders twice a week each summer on a six-day
adventure to Halfway Lodge. No previous riding experience is required for

this slow ride that will redefine your relationship with the backcountry.

Relax, pardner, there's no trotting, cantering, or galloping. Banff Trail Riders' three-hundred-strong stable of horses and mules largely come from auctions; animals rescued and patiently trained for excursions that range from hour-long joyrides to epic adventures. Either way, the pace is gentle but steady, the horses responsive and sure-footed, and the views guaranteed. Meeting my fellow

riders at the stable, I am also introduced to my gelding, Lakota, and our trusty if eccentric pack mule, Aardvark. Over the next six days, I will get to know many unique personalities, both equine and human. Riding western style, our patient guide instructs us how to lean forward in the saddle when going uphill, how to lean back when going downhill, and the importance of standing on stirrups when our horses take a pee break. We get the hang of it real fast, and riding horses this calm and well-trained allows us to tune into our surroundings and truly immerse ourselves in the beauty of our surroundings.

Out and back from the Banff townsite, we will visit two mountain lodges en route to our destination, the 2,440-metre-high Allenby Pass. After a four-hour ride, and having stopped for a lunch of grilled steaks over firewood, I stiffly dismount Lakota at the Sundance Lodge. We'd long left behind cell service and there's no Wi-Fi, just a welcome party of fat, hoary marmots. The lodge has comfy beds, hot showers and flush toilets, sofas, wood stoves, and a tireless, talented chef. Yes, my knees and

butt are on the verge of mutiny, but painkillers and Pinot Noir help, along with the support of fellow riders hailing from across Canada, the U.S., Australia, and the U.K. When you disconnect from the news, email, and social media, you instantly connect with the people, landscape, and modest options around you. Suddenly there's time to pick a book from the shelf, rope a wood steer, stargaze, learn a card game, and listen to the stories of your new companions.

Mule packers collect our bags early in the morning to transport them up ahead. After breakfast, we load up our saddlebags, mount our steeds, and amble into the wild. When you walk you must look ahead, especially on a challenging trail with thick mud, slippery roots, horse manure, and sharp rocks. Horses take all this in their stride, allowing riders to gaze into the trees, down the valleys, along the creeks, and up the peaks. Through dense pines, fir, spruce, and wild shrubs, we progress across clear-water creeks and narrow switchbacks. It's another long day in the saddle, but our reward is the century-old Halfway Lodge, facing one of the most magnificent views in the country.

The cozy, two-storey, four-bedroom lodge serves as base camp for three days of off-grid mountain wonderland. Everything is packed in by mule: the propane gas for heating and hot showers, the food that a solitary chef will spoil you with, the warm flannel linen, towels, and horse supplies. With mules arriving only every couple of days from Banff, over thirty-two kilometres away, the unhurried stillness is quite literally a breath of fresh air. We don't need much: it's fine to wear the same clothes every day, and slickers are provided to keep us dry if the weather turns sour. There's no electricity, but camera phones can go far on airplane mode, and a portable charger sees me through.

The impact of riding above the treeline, surrounded by an amphitheatre of dramatic limestone peaks is indescribable, so I won't bother. Words like "goosebumps" and "wow" are, however, typical, along with prayers of gratitude to whatever deity one credits for the opportunity to be one of only about two hundred people who visit the pass each year. One thing is certain: you recognize a bucket-list moment when you have it, and trust me, you will have it on Allenby Pass.

The following day, we leave the horses behind and take a steep hike up along a creek to Lake Matthias. It's our own private Lake Louise, a gemstone-hued, glacier-fed marvel cradled by sharp peaks, rock scree, and virgin forest. I recharge my off-grid soul with a swim its icy, drinkable water, grateful there's a warm, late-summer sun to dry me off. Returning to the lodge, I count a half-dozen waterfalls and over two dozen species of mushroom. We feast that night, play cribbage, and toast the highlights in a weekend full of them.

Our group returns along the same path that brought us here, arriving for our final night in Sundance Lodge, weathered and tired. As riders, and as people, my group has bonded in those mountains, through conversation and quiet periods of introspection along the trail. Closer to town, we join up with two front-country riding groups, the short excursions that welcome hordes of visitors each summer. Riding single file, it's rush hour all the way back to the stables, a poignant reminder that multiday trail riding represents a vastly different — and entirely unforgettable — bucket-list experience.

FEAST IN A MEDIEVAL ENCAMPMENT

A knight to remember

📍 Three Hills

🔗 canadianbucketlist.com/medievalglamping

WHAT HO! GATHER YE DAMSELS AND POLISH YE SWORDS, FOR by my troth there lies a medieval encampment burrowed into the rolling green hills of southern Alberta-land. Tallyho, it is time to dress, feast, and joust like royalty.

About an hour's drive from Calgary, Good Knights is a one-of-a-kind medieval-themed glamping experience. Something this strange and marvellous only comes about through unbridled passion. Allow me to introduce Sir Daniel and Lady Linda Smith: retirees, Dungeons & Dragons devotees, dreamers. Originally from Calgary, the Smiths fell in love with medieval Europe and each other as teenagers on a high-school trip. Thus began a fruitful union that resulted in children, careers (environmental consulting and human resources), and a lifelong passion for medieval swordplay, armour, fairs, archery, and costumes.

Medieval-themed fairs and events take place around the world, and the Smiths travelled to overnight fairs and delighted townsfolk with their luxurious, royal tent. Upon retirement, Linda wondered if they could offer the opulent medieval environment to others. Daniel, a sprightly man with unlimited energy, pounced on the dream. Having already relocated to a quiet twenty-acre site outside of Three Hills, Alberta, they got to work.

Inspired by the aesthetic of an African safari tent, they built theirs with wooden floors and ensuite bathrooms, comfortable beds, and cozy, era-specific furnishings. They also constructed an ambitious six-hundred-square-foot *Hobbit*-inspired burrow, built directly into the hill, with five furnished rooms, a cedar hot tub, circular doorways, and a living roof. Like many retirees, the Smiths found themselves working harder than ever: raising the money, figuring out the construction, getting the permits, and opening for business. Volunteers and bannermen helped out, and a local costume enthusiast provided dozens of costumes for all ages. Activities like swordplay, traditional dancing, archery, and storytelling would keep guests busy, although it's enough to roam about under that big prairie sky, robed like a princess or squire.

Thanks to enthusiastic town criers, Good Knights is typically booked all the summer, hosting wedding parties, families, students, and anyone with an imaginative penchant for lyre music and feasts. You don't have

to be a fan of *The Lord of the Rings*, *Game of Thrones*, Harry Potter, or Robin Hood, but if you are, you're going to *love* this.

As my six-year-old and I arrive at Good Knights' wooden fortress gates, I half expect horns to sound and foot soldiers to appear on the turrets, taunting us like the mischievous French knights in *Monty Python and the Holy Grail*. Instead, we're greeted by the affable Sir Daniel, who shows us to our accommodation: a custom-built *vardo* — a wagon for travelling minstrels. Like the tents, the *vardo* has power, a latrine, a sink, ample storage space, and a queen-size mattress draped in colourful blankets. We're ushered to the costume shed to select our style:

royalty, warrior, or peasant? Furnished in leather and cloth, we meet the weekend townsfolk, which include a group of young teachers from Edmonton, a family from Calgary, and a combined stag/stagette party.

"We seem to book more and more of those," explains Sir Daniel. Mind you, these are not clubbing-dancing-fall-down-drunk stags. Good Knights attracts gentle folks who have more than enough fun dressing up, sharing tales around a campfire, and playing obscure games like Pegs and Jokers. There's still plenty of ale to go around.

"The guests are the best part," confirms Lady Linda, joining us for coffee after single-handedly preparing a fantastic breakfast. This is even more remarkable given the fact that she uses a wheelchair due to polio (the encampment is proudly accessible for others with mobility issues). Later, we walk up the hill to catch a marvellous prairie view, then my son practises his axe-tossing (not real axes), archery, and sword-fighting skills with Sir Daniel (real and wooden swords).

Noble feasts are included in overnight weekend packages, taking place Saturday nights in the Grand Hall. Knightly tales are shared over goblets of ale and wooden plates with Irish soda bread, soup, meats, and vegetables. Later that night, I watch satellites float across the sky, warmed by a thick hooded cloak.

The Encampment operates four months a year, with the self-catered Burrow open year-round. Business is brisk, but given the small team running everything behind the scenes, Sir Daniel tells me there are no plans to expand. Nine themed tents can accommodate between thirty and forty people, which is exactly the way they like it. That said, the *vardo* is something new, and more wagons might well find themselves rolling into the Encampment.

As harbingers for the exciting new world of themed glamping, let us praise Good Knights for their passion, hospitality, and courage to take up the gauntlet.

FLOW WITH THE BOW

An urban float experience

📍 Calgary

🔗 canadianbucketlist.com/lazyday

WE HAVE ALREADY ESTABLISHED THAT FLOATING DOWN A river on a tube is a splendid activity (see "Float a River Channel," pages 86–88). We have also established that floating down a river without a tube can be a bucket-list activity too (see "Snorkel with Salmon," pages 36–38). Here's one more, similar in principle and yet uniquely different from either.

With glacial headwaters in the Rockies, the Bow River travels through Banff, Canmore, Cochrane, and Calgary. Farther up in the mountains, it invites traditional whitewater rafting adventures, navigating steep canyons and bone-drenching rapids. By the time the Bow reaches Calgary, the current remains swift but the rapids have subsided. On sunny days from June to September, it becomes the site of one of Cowtown's most popular summer activities.

You don't need to be a local, or own a raft or tube. Operating out of the Calgary Curling Club, Lazy Day Raft Rentals makes it easy: rent a custom inflatable raft, kayak, or tube; hop on the shuttle to the West Baker Park boat launch; jump in your raft; get into the flow; and let the current return to sender. Most one-way trips take between two and four hours, but you can keep the raft all day, swishing up to beaches and sandbanks along the way. Rafts can accommodate between four and twelve people, and while the Bow is surprisingly clear for a major urban waterway, swimming is not advised due to industrial activities, stormwater, and the city's wastewater treatment. No bother: lie back, soak up the sunshine, waving to locals on the riverbank, drifting under various bridges, and relishing a distinctly natural experience in a distinctly urban setting.

LEARN SOMETHING NEW

Hitting the cross-cultural bull's eye

📍 Mountain View County

🔗 canadianbucketlist.com/paintedwarriors

I'M SITTING AROUND A CAMPFIRE, WATCHING SPRUCE LOGS burn, doing what one does when the world stops for half a minute. When the phone stops ringing, emails don't avalanche, and there's nothing to do but sit, think, and chat. Aspens tremble in the breeze, wood cracks, and birds form a choir. The topic: What does it mean

to have an Indigenous experience? To connect with our home *on*
native land?

There's a lot of curiosity and demand out there: Growth in the
Indigenous tourism sector has outpaced overall Canadian tourism
activity, attracting both foreign and local visitors to diverse activities
and destinations across the country. There are heritage parks and pow-
wow events, fishing lodges, protected historical sites, and busy urban art
galleries. And then there's Painted Warriors, an eighty-two-acre ranch in
the Rocky Mountain foothills.

Earlier, Tracey Klettl showed me how to nock my arrow, clipping it to
the line of my compound bow, and resting it in the wonderfully-named
whisker biscuit. Familiarizing myself with archery's lingo, it felt a lot
like golf: success comes down to gear, technique, practice, and mental
acuity. Tracey explained that the dominant eye is more important in
marksmanship than the dominant hand. Turns out I've been aiming
incorrectly all my life, relying on the wrong eye (I'm right-handed but
left-eyed). Switching my bow to the opposite hand, she advised me to

loosen my grip and compress my shoulder blades. Now I fired the arrow relatively straight, although the life-size animal target figurines in the forest could rest easy. Tracey's partner, Tim Mearns, pulled out his bow, and pegged the tiny head of a golf tee over fifty yards away. If I ever have to hunt for my food, I really hope they're around. Not only are they certified hunting, archery, outdoor skills, and horse-riding coaches, they're competitive archery champions too.

"Technology really comes between us and the natural world," says Tracey now, peering into the fire. Adds Tim, nursing a cup of coffee: "If you take your shoes and socks off and stand on the earth, you can feel a charge." Painted Warriors was initially founded to educate and certify trail-riding, hunting, and outdoor-adventure guides. For Tracey and Tim, it was crucial to approach their work through an Indigenous lens. Tracey is of Cree and Mohawk descent from what is now Jasper National Park. Tim is Saulteaux and a member of the Cote First Nation in Saskatchewan. Proud and knowledgeable of their heritage, they welcome groups of Indigenous kids and adults, many of whom have lost touch with both outdoor skills and the spiritual component that accompanies them.

They tell me about the significance of smudging, laying tobacco, honouring the harvested animals, and using all parts of the animal to respect their sacrifice. They also invite my questions and curiosity. What's the story behind the large elk head above the gift shop door? Do you stalk or ambush animals on the bow hunt? Where is an ethical kill shot, and why is it so important?

With six large canvas tents open year-round, the couple quickly realized the potential to offer tourism experiences beyond guide training. Today, guests visit from around the world, engaging their senses through half-day interpretative forest walks, horseback riding (from introductory rides to a ten-day Horseback Adventure), archery,

MORE INDIGENOUS ALBERTA

Métis Crossing, Smoky Lake: Located on the shores of the North Saskatchewan River, Métis Crossing is an interpretive centre on the original river lots of the province's Métis settlers. Among the exhibits, programs, and activities, visitors can learn to set beaver traps, sample dried bison, and immerse themselves in Métis history and traditions.

Blackfoot Crossing Historical Park: An hour's drive south of Calgary, interactive exhibits guide visitors into the history, language, and culture of the Siksika Nation. Catch dance and craft demonstrations, camp overnight in an on-site tipi, learn traditional survival skills, and sample traditional Indigenous food at the restaurant.

Head-Smashed-In Buffalo Jump: This UNESCO World Heritage Site is the most significant and best-preserved buffalo jump site on the continent. An excellent interpretive centre offers exhibits and guided tours, and presentations provide insights into the traditional methods used by Indigenous hunters, the ecological significance of North American bison, and the cultural significance of the site.

Writing-on-Stone/Áísínai'pi: Certified as a UNESCO World Heritage Site in 2019, Writing-on-Stone park contains the greatest concentration of rock art on the Great Plains of North America. Over a thousand pieces of art have been found in the park. Take a tour of the rock art or a walk among the striking hoodoos, or sign up for storytelling and other cultural programs.

winter snowshoe experiences, and craft workshops. Infused throughout are the traditions, stories, and customs of their Cree, Ojibway, and Métis culture. In the forest, Tracey explains how white powder on aspen trees functions as a compass, and also an effective sunblock (good for SPF 15). She reveals how her grandmother, passing on her medicine-woman knowledge of land and plants, used wild strawberries to treat upset stomachs, and wild rose for eye infections. Even weeds like plantago can be chewed up and used to treat wasp stings.

"There are no weeds in Indigenous culture," explains Tracey, who credits her sister Brenda as the knowledge keeper in the family. Brenda offers Medicine Walks in Banff and Sundre through her own outfit, Mahikan Trails.

With their warmth, honesty, hospitality, and humour, it's clear that Painted Warriors is more than just archery, hunting, forest glamping, and the healing properties of plants. It's an opportunity to engage with Indigenous culture and traditions in a beautiful environment and an inviting, safe space. We all come from different backgrounds, and we anchor ourselves with different opinions. Yet different cultures have so much more in common than we realize. We all want to be safe, inspired, and content. We all want the best for our children, and to do the right thing. Take it from someone who's visited over a hundred countries and chatted with locals from Albania to Zanzibar: it's the people you meet who create the paradise you find.

ROCK OUT AT STUDIO BELL

Canada's jam-packed musical journey

📍 Calgary

🔗 canadianbucketlist.com/cmhf

FROM LEONARD COHEN, BTO, AND JONI MITCHELL TO BRYAN Adams, Justin Bieber, and Drake, Canada's contribution to the global music industry has been extraordinary. Celebrating this legacy along with the cultural impact of music, Calgary's Studio Bell houses the National Music Centre and Canadian Music Hall of Fame. Five floors of exhibitions showcase Canadian musical icons, along with interactive installations, workshops, instrument showcases, and fascinating memorabilia. Jam along to the hits, and let the (Canadian) beat play on and on.

ALBERTA

RACE THE FAMILY

It's all downhill from here

📍 Calgary
🔗 canadianbucketlist.com/downhillkarting

CREDIT INGENIOUS NEW ZEALANDERS FOR INVENTING A unique go-cart ride that will thrill the entire family. Located at the WinSport Canada Olympic Park, Downhill Karting puts you in an easy-to-operate wheeled cart that uses gravity to roll down a 1,800-metre twisting, purpose-built track. Kids as young as six can ride their own cart (younger kids can sit in your lap), and riders can blitz down as fast as their nerves allow. A modified ski chair ushers both riders and carts to the top of the hill. There are various packages available, but four rides should satiate your need for speed.

PROTECT A WOLF-DOG

Keep your pups at home

⊗ Cochrane
⊘ canadianbucketlist.com/yamnuska

OVER THE COURSE OF MILLENNIA, VARIOUS TRAITS WERE slowly bred out of the wolf, reducing the canine's natural aggression, size, shyness, mottled coat, and territorial instinct. Today's labradoodles, cockapoos, chihuahuas, boxers, and bulldogs have come a long way. Siberian huskies and Alaskan malamutes, while looking a bit like a wolf, are in fact pure dog, all *Canis familiaris* with no *Canis lupus.* Then you get the wolf-dog.

A mix of wolf and dog, the hybrid species shares traits of both. Wolf-dogs are controversially bred as exotic pets for people who typically have no idea what they're getting themselves into. Wolf-dogs make terrible pets. They tend to be aggressive, destructive, and unpredictable, and show a strong drive to hunt. They need large, secure enclosures, raw-meat diets, and specialized veterinary care. Graded according to how much wolf they exhibit in their appearance, behaviour, and DNA, even low-content wolf-dogs — with approximately 20 to 49 percent wolf — can be a handful, and dodgy breeders often misrepresent this content to encourage sales. High-content wolf-dogs — 80 to 95 percent wolf — are essentially wild animals. Many provinces have banned the sale or breeding of wolf-dogs, while others, including Alberta, allow wolf-dog ownership without special permits (although some municipalities have taken matters into their own hands, banning wolf-dogs regardless). Unfortunately, wolf-dogs continue to be irresponsibly bred and bought, abandoned, rescued, or brought to pounds (where they are likely to be euthanized). Nobody *needs* a wolf-dog, the way nobody *needs* a tiger. They're fearful of humans, and with their strong pack mentality, they can be dangerous around kids and strangers outside the pack. Wolf-dogs simply have not evolved for belly scratches, pet treats, or doggie parks.

Located about halfway between Calgary and Banff, the Yamnuska Wolf-dog Sanctuary outside the town of Cochrane is doing its best to help. With forty-three permanent residents in seventeen packs, Yamnuska was founded in 2011 to raise public awareness about both wolf-dogs and wolves, and create a safe haven for abandoned, rescued, and donated wolf-dogs. Visitors stroll through a lovely wooded sanctuary, peering into fenced enclosures for glimpses of the packs, educating themselves through interpretative signs along the way. Trainers invite questions as they pop inside various enclosures throughout the day. An interactive tour allows visitors fifteen years and older to enter two enclosures under the guidance of a trainer, where they learn all about wolf-dogs while engaging with some of the more approachable members of the Yamnuska family. "If you are scared of big dogs, this tour is not for you," advises the website.

I'm struck by the wolf-dogs' physical appearance: their lean legs, thick chest, and shedding

fur. Some seem more doglike than others, but plenty of warning signs remind me these are wild animals with very sharp teeth. A wolf-dog stalks my six-year-old as we walk along the sanctuary path. My son thinks it's a fun game with a friendly dog, but I wouldn't bet the farmhouse that's what's actually going on.

I leave the centre inspired by the work of its staff, volunteers, and supporters, yet saddened that a sanctuary like this has to exist in the first place. How is it still legal to breed and possess hybrid, dangerous animals for the sake of human enjoyment? If and when wolf-dogs are finally illegal, the centre hopes to transform into a wolf sanctuary, dispelling the big, bad myths about an important and fascinating apex predator. In the meantime, centuries of breeding and loyal companionship will ensure your border collie, dachshund, golden retriever, Pomeranian, Yorkshire terrier, or other friendly pup appreciates your food *and* your company.

ENCOUNTER VERY BIG THINGS

Now that's a roadside attraction

🔗 canadianbucketlist.com/bigthings

AT SOME POINT IN THE DISTANT PAST, SOMEBODY DECIDED TO build a very big thing.

"If we build a big thing," they said, holding a cold beer at the pub, "people will stop on their way through town, take a picture, and maybe spend some money."

"This is an interesting proposition," said Somebody's best mate, who happened to own the town's sole grocer/gas station/post office/haberdashery. "How big does it have to be?"

"Oh," replied Somebody, already getting ideas in his head, "positively gigantic. In fact, it needs to be the biggest thing in the world!"

Thanks to these dreamers, road trippers around the world often and quite unexpectedly stumble upon a Very Big Thing. If you're driving around Alberta, this is all but guaranteed: the province has over *one hundred* of them. You'll need the World's Largest Western Boot in Edmonton to squash the World's Largest Dragonfly south of Wabamun. The World's Largest Railway Spike in Hines Creek might come in handy fending off the World's Largest Dinosaur in Drumheller. Golfers will want to swing past the nine-hole Bow Island Golf Club to find the World's Largest Putter, but you'll have to drive 330-kilometres north to Trochu to find the World's Largest Golf Tee. The World's Largest Chuckwagon (Dewberry), the World's Largest Mushrooms (Vilna), the Biggest Piggy Bank in the World (Coleman), the World's Largest Mallard Duck (Andrew), the World's Largest Sausage (Mundare) — there's clearly a lot of Somebodies in Alberta committed to going big. Any road trip in the province is richer for their quirky efforts.

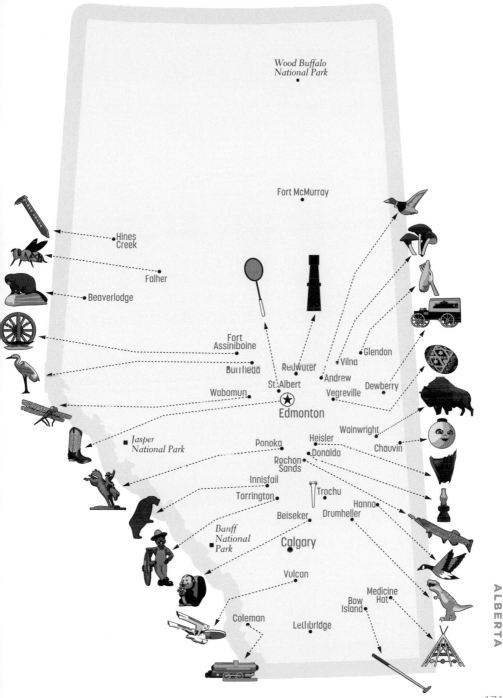

Wood Buffalo
National Park

Fort McMurray

Hines
Creek

Falher

Beaverlodge

Fort
Assiniboine

Barrhead   Redwater

Wabamun   St. Albert   Andrew

Edmonton   Vegreville

Glendon

Vilna

Dewberry

Wainwright

Jasper
National Park

Ponoka   Heisler

Donalda   Chauvin

Rochon
Sands

Innisfail

Torrington   Trochu

Beiseker   Drumheller   Hanna

Banff
National
Park   Calgary

Vulcan

Bow
Island   Medicine
Hat

Coleman   Lethbridge

BEAM YOURSELF TO VULCAN

Boldly go where people have gone before

📍 Vulcan

🔗 canadianbucketlist.com/vulcan

ARE YOU PREPARED TO BOLDLY GO WHERE NO ONE HAS GONE
before? Me neither, which is why I took a detour south of Calgary to the
town of Vulcan, cleverly capitalizing on its name to become a cosmic
attraction in the fanatical *Star Trek* universe. It's worth pointing out
that *Star Trek* has many Canadian connections: the first-ever episode
aired in Canada first on September 6, 1966; the Canadian Mint created
special coins for *Star Trek*'s fiftieth anniversary; "Spocking" became a
brief thing in 2015, whereby a few lines drawn on the five-dollar bill

UFO LANDING PAD

In 1967, the town of St. Paul, Alberta, unveiled the World's First UFO Landing Pad, officially welcoming all aliens and spaceships to use the spaceport. If they need to stretch their legs or find some snacks for the time warp, they can pop into the adjacent Tourist Information Centre for a latte and boutique artisan gifts. All species are welcome.

transformed Sir Wilfrid Laurier, legally, into Mr. Spock. *Star Trek* films and TV series have been shot in Vancouver and Toronto, and featured Canadian actors in iconic roles like Scotty (James Doohan was born and raised in Vancouver), *Picard*'s Alison Pill, General Chang (Christopher Plummer), and all sorts of Klingons and *Enterprise* crew. William Shatner, of course, is from Montreal, because it would have been too damn weird if he was born and raised in Vulcan.

A community association launched Vulcan's *Star Trek* connection in 1991, although road trippers had been stopping to take pictures of the town's concrete sign for decades. In 1998, a ten-metre-long replica starship *Enterprise* was placed outside the distinctly spaceship-looking Vulcan Tourism & Trek Station. Inside you'll find over eight hundred pieces of *Star Trek* memorabilia, swishing doors, costumes, and Spock ears in the gift shop. There's also a transporter on Centre Street, a bust of Leonard Nimoy on the corner of Second Avenue, and other quirks that Trekkies will appreciate when exploring the town. Vulcan hosts an annual *Star Trek* gathering called Vul-Con, bringing enthusiasts and cast and crew members together, including the late Leonard Nimoy, who attended in 2010. Located less than an hour and a half's drive from Calgary, it's highly illogical — as Spock might say — for a small prairie town in Alberta to become intrinsically linked to one of the most popular science fiction franchises of all time. Captain Picard might add: "Things are only impossible until they're not." Enjoy your visit, live long, and prosper.

SEE A GOPHER DIORAMA

For the squirrel-brained

⚲ Torrington
🔗 canadianbucketlist.com/gopher

GAZING AT FORTY-FOUR DIORAMAS CONTAINING STUFFED
ground squirrels in human clothes is not, I confess, your typical goose-bumping, peak-of-life experience. It is however bizarre, unique, a great story, and let's face it, morbidly hilarious. Like these burrowing rodents, the town of Torrington has seen better days. With little industry and

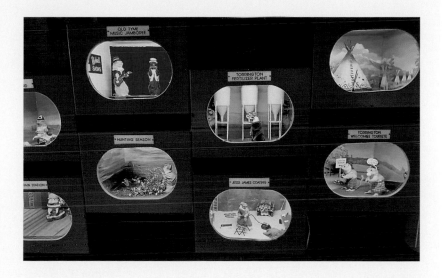

fields overrun with furry critters, what could possibly attract visitors to veer off Highway 2 between Calgary and Red Deer? In the spirit of big Albertan thinking, someone on council suggested they stuff the damn gophers — technically Richardson's ground squirrels — and make a museum out of them. In 1996, the Gopher Hole Museum opened its doors, and ten thousand people showed up that year. Town volunteers used props, found objects, and doll clothing to position the squirrels in delightful scenes from a small town, with quirky comment cards. "Oh boy, am I ever stuffed!" says one unfortunate fella at the dinner table. There's the barbershop, the blacksmith, the beauty salon, the curling rink, a yard sale, and romance in the moonlight too. Each diorama depicts an element of humour and fun, but also a deep sense of nostalgia and longing too. Time is a cruel mistress, unless you're an erroneously-identified rodent, frozen in a small-town museum for posterity. The World Famous Gopher Hole Museum is located about an hour and fifteen minutes' drive from Calgary, or fifty minutes south from Red Deer. Entrance is by much-appreciated donation.

EPILOGUE

MY BUCKET LIST BEGAN WITH AN ACCIDENT. A CAR RAN A stop sign in downtown Vancouver, plowed into my bike, and broke my kneecap. It was just the sort of brush with mortality I needed to remind myself there was so much I wanted to do, and so little time to do it. I quit my job, cashed in a twenty-thousand-dollar insurance settlement, bought a round-the-world ticket, and set out to tick off my bucket list. Twelve months and twenty-four countries later, I returned home with the realization that bucket lists grow and evolve like the rest of us. Two decades and over a hundred countries later, I'm still writing new ones. Like a game of Whac-A-Mole, if you tick one item off at the top, another three pop up at the bottom.

The people we meet create the paradise we find, and it is they who shade the colours of our journey. My single biggest piece of advice for any of these experiences: share them with company you enjoy, and if you're on your own, be open and friendly to those around you. Travelling is as personal as the wear and tear on your toothbrush. You will likely encounter an altogether different experience when you tick these experiences off. How you end up exploring Western Canada will ultimately be as unique as you are, even if it's only by reading the pages of this book.

While *The Great Western Canada Bucket List* introduces a variety of experiences, I'm well aware there are woeful omissions, items known and less-known that I haven't got to just yet. Visit canadianbucketlist.com and let me know what they are. This second edition features *double* the experiences in the first, because the more we dig, the more we find, and the more we find, the more stories we create to relish and share. Grizzly bear viewing, whale-watching, hiking with bison, luxury tree houses, one-of-a-kind restaurants and hotels — it seems there's always more to discover.

ACKNOWLEDGEMENTS

THIS BUCKET LIST IS THE RESULT OF MANY MILES AND MANY years of travel, with the professional and personal help of many people and organizations. My deep gratitude to all below, along with all the airlines, ferries, trains, buses, hotels, B&Bs, and organizations who assisted me along the way.

British Columbia: Destination British Columbia, Sabrina Robson, Caroline Mongrain, Nathalie Gauthier, Janice Greenwood-Fraser, Jacqueline Simpson, Andrea Visscher, Lana Kingston, Susan Hubbard, Liz Sperandeo, Darryl Lenuik, Teresa Davis, Josie Heisig, Luba Plotnikoff, Geoff Moore, Heidi Korven, Cindy Burr, Mika Ryan, Nancie Hall, BC Ferries, Barb Scott, Howard Grieve, Ellen Walker-Matthews, Morgan Sommerville, Holly Wood, Robin Baycroft, Dee Raffo, Stacy Chala, Carly Moran, Sarah Pearson, Jeremy Roche, CMH Heli-Skiing, Brian Peech, Greg McCracken, Amber Sessions, Jorden Hutchison, Sonu Purhar, Tourism Vancouver, Randy Burke, David Suzuki, Feet Banks, Monica Dickinson, Jeff Topham, EagleRider Vancouver, Great Canadian Trails, Masa Takei, Stephanie Lewis, Jordan Trustham, Michael Hannan, Rusty Noble, Juliette Recompsat, Holly Lenk, Karly Upshall, Angeline Chew, Katie Dabbs, Lee Newman, TJ Watt, Rob Feakins, and Shereen Abbas.

Alberta: Travel Alberta, Tourism Calgary, Parks Canada, Michelle Gaudet, Aviva Kohen, Brynn Parker, Cathy Lawton, Jessica Harcombe-Fleming, Anastasia Martin-Stilwell, Amy Wolski, Hala Dehais, Vanessa Gagnon, Charlie Locke, Tricia Woikin, Mary Morrison, Tessa Mackay,

Doug Lentz, Go RVing, Nancy Dery, Bin Lau, Ralph Sliger, Ian Mackenzie, Ashley Meller, Banff Trail Riders, Paul Vance, Sean Cable, Eric Magnon, and Guy Theriault.

Special Thanks: The wonderful team at Dundurn Press: Kathryn Lane, Kwame Scott Fraser, Kendra Martin, Meghan Macdonald, Ankit Pahwa, and Elena Radic. Jess Shulman did the impossible job of filtering my bad lines and somehow fitting this all into a single volume. Laura Boyle completely overhauled the design to make this book pop off your coffee table. Several of these stories appeared in different form across multiple publications. My thanks to Alexandra Pope, Madigan Cotterill, Sarah Brown, Sam Burkhart, and Zebunnisa Mirza. My gratitude to the Royal Canadian Geographical Society, and all at *Canadian Geographic*. A tip of the bucket list to David Rock, Jon Rothbart, Ian Mackenzie, Sean Aiken, Gary Kalmek, Joe Kalmek, Bradley Kalmek, Heather Taylor, Elyse Mailhot, Linda Bates, Gloria Loree, Ernst Flach, Kate Rogers, Deirdre Campbell, Destination Canada, Diane Selkirk, Ken Hegan, Rob Baron, Jarrod Levitan, the Vancouver and Burnaby Public Libraries, Sherrill Sirrs, Chris Lee, the Heights family, and my dear Kalmeks for their unconditional support. My gratitude and respect to every bookseller and tourism business no doubt working themselves to the bone, enduring endless challenges with an unshakeable belief in the power of words and experience. And finally, to Ana, Raquel, and Galileo — where in the world would I be without you?

IMAGE CREDITS

Bottlescrew Bills, courtesy of, 115

Bray, Ryan, courtesy of Parks Canada, 122

Bride, Paul, courtesy of Sea to Sky Gondola, 97

Butchart Gardens, courtesy of, 52

Capilano Suspension Bridge, courtesy of, vi, 61, 63

Cassell, Amanda Hudson, courtesy of Pursuit, 59

Cypress Mountain, courtesy of, 66

Esrock, Ana, 27

Esrock, Galileo, 48

Esrock, Robin, 8, 11, 13, 14, 15, 18, 19, 28, 31, 32, 33, 34, 37, 43, 46, 51, 64, 65, 71, 74, 76, 77, 83, 84, 86, 87, 89, 91, 94, 98, 112, 119, 124, 125, 137, 138, 140, 151, 152, 154, 158, 159, 160, 161, 164, 165, 172, 174, 175

Esrocking the World Media Inc., 1, 4, 21, 93, 107, 147, 149, 171

Explore Edmonton, courtesy of, 136

Fairmont Hotels and Resorts, courtesy of, 44

Feakins, Rob, 68, 70

Good Knights, courtesy of, 156

Gowans, Emi, vii, 150

Harris, Alyx, courtesy of Yamnuska Wolfdog Sanctuary, 167, 169

iStock, 36, 57, 58, 88, 109, 132, 146

ITAC, courtesy of, 163

Kalmek, Joe, 127

Koreski, Jeremy, courtesy of Tourism Tofino, 25

Leniuk, Darryl, 103

Mackenzie, Ian, 113

McGee, Craig, courtesy of CMH, 39

Moore, Geoff, 79

Moraine Lake Lodge, courtesy of, 128, 129

Newman, Lee, 22

Pixabay, 123, 133

Pursuit, courtesy of, 62, 67, 142

Riff Stills, courtesy of Tourism Sun Peaks, 108

Rocky Mountaineer, courtesy of, 144

Scuccato, Alex, courtesy of Explore Edmonton, 134

Sea Vancouver, courtesy of, 60

Seehagel, Mike, courtesy of Pursuit, 130

Ski Big 3, courtesy of, 116

Sunshine Coast Tourism, courtesy of, 85

Superfly, courtesy of Esrocking the World Media Inc., 56

Teron, Chase, courtesy of Klahoose Wilderness Resort, 78

Topham, Jeff, 81, 143

Tourism Calgary, courtesy of, 166

Tourism Jasper, courtesy of, 141

Vail Resorts, courtesy of, 54

Villagomez, Dennis, 29

Watt, TJ/Ancient Forest Alliance, 47, 49

White, Brad, courtesy of CMH, 41

Whitfield, Aaron, courtesy of NE Heli Skiing, 72, 99, 100

Williamson, Connie, courtesy of Tourism Sun Peaks, 104

INDEX

Illustrations indicated by page numbers in italics

ABOUT THE AUTHOR

Photo by Jeff Topham

Robin Esrock is an author, journalist, TV host, columnist, and public speaker. He is the author of the smash bestselling book series the Great Canadian Bucket List, along with several international bestsellers. Robin's stories and photography have appeared in major publications on five continents, including *National Geographic Traveler*, the *Guardian, Chicago Tribune*, the *Globe and Mail*, and *Canadian Geographic*. The creator and co-host of the internationally syndicated television series *Word Travels*, Robin has been widely profiled as a "bucket list" travel expert, and his TEDx travel talk has over one million views. Robin lives with his family in Vancouver, B.C. Catch up with him at robinesrock.com or canadianbucketlist.com.